This book is a nonmathematical overview of decision theory. It presents the logic of rationality and the basics of the theory of games. It shows how social choice theory yields a parallel logic, a logic of choosing for others. It considers the part that is played by how people grasp or *see* their situations, how different *seeings* can make for ambiguity and for inner conflicts and value reversals – and how these can be dealt with. And it discusses some problems of time: problems of discounting, of value change, and of the contingency of our future values on what we do today. The author presents many examples from history and from literature, examples dealing with love, war, friendship, and crime.

This is a short book with much breadth of scope. It will interest anyone concerned with the problems of decision making, whether in philosophy, psychology, or economics.

MAKING CHOICES

Making Choices

A Recasting of Decision Theory

FREDERIC SCHICK

CAMBRIDGE
UNIVERSITY PRESS

PUBLISHED BY THE PRESS SYNDICATE OF THE UNIVERSITY OF CAMBRIDGE
The Pitt Building, Trumpington Street, Cambridge CB2 1RP, United Kingdom

CAMBRIDGE UNIVERSITY PRESS
The Edinburgh Building, Cambridge CB2 2RU, UK http: //www.cup.cam.ac.uk
40 West 20th Street, New York, NY 10011-4211, USA http: //www.cup.org
10 Stamford Road, Oakleigh, Melbourne 3166, Australia

First published 1997
Reprinted 1998

Printed in the United States of America

Typeset in Meridien

A catalogue record for this book is available from the British Library

Library of Congress Catalogue card number: 84-23807

ISBN 0-521-58181-8 hardback
ISBN 0-521-58840-5 paperback

CONTENTS

1

DIFFICULT CHOICES

LIFE is a long trip in a cheap car. In a dark country. Without a good map. Not knowing the roads, we must stop at each fork to make a decision, to choose in some way. How well, in the end, we think the trip went depends on how well we chose. But choosing is often difficult.

1 SCOUNDREL TIME

Suppose you are under heavy pressure to bring certain charges against your friends. You know that your friends have done no wrong, but that your making these charges against them would cause them a lot of trouble. Suppose, if you didn't, you might go to jail, that you would certainly lose your job, perhaps your career and your future. What are you going to do? In the early 1950s, many people had to ask themselves this. It wasn't an idle question for them. They knew that any day they might be called on for their answer.

For Lillian Hellman, the day arrived in February of 1952. A subpoena had come from Washington, from the House Committee on Un-American Activities, a summons like those many other writers and artists had already received. She was invited to testify, to answer questions about her political views and about those of others, to say that this or that person had once belonged to some leftist group or been at some socialist meeting or contributed to some left-leaning fund. None of this was against the law, and she knew many such people. But if she mentioned any of them, they would be in serious trouble. If she refused, she could be held in contempt of Congress, in which case she would be jailed. She might explain her refusal to speak by pleading the Fifth Amendment, saying that her testimony could incriminate her. That would take her off the hook, but it would mean to the press and the public that she was guilty of a crime.

She was, she writes, in "a sweat of bewilderment," determined not to take part in a witch hunt, but panicked also at the thought of prison. The rights and wrongs were obvious to her. She thought of the members of the Committee as scoundrels, as sleazy opportunists. She saw them engaged in an inquisition indifferent to truth and to decency. She knew that she had to resist these people. Still, though the call of principle was clear, the voice of prudence also made itself heard. Jail would be hard to take. And she was of course aware that prudence often shames principle. She couldn't be sure she would stand her ground. Other witnesses, as angry as she, had turned in the end and run for cover.

In this frame of mind, she consulted Abe Fortas, then a lawyer in private practice, many years still from joining the Supreme Court. Fortas thought that "the time had come . . . for somebody to take a moral position . . . , to say, in essence, I will testify about myself, answer all your questions about my own life, but I will not tell you about anybody else, stranger or friend."[1] This suggested a new approach, but it would be risky. If the Committee refused to allow it, she could no longer plead the Fifth Amendment. Having offered to talk about herself would imply she had nothing to hide. That would keep her from saying that talking about others could incriminate her.

Hellman seized on Fortas's suggestion. Here would be some dignity, some show of proper resistance; at least she wouldn't rat on her friends. When she appeared before the Committee, she made her offer and the Committee rejected it. After that, she refused to answer questions. How she avoided a contempt citation never fully came clear.

What made Hellman's issue so difficult? I have reported the problem she had as an inner conflict, as a conflict of prudence and principle, a conflict of her self-interest and the principles she lived by. This, however, puts it badly, for her principles were *part* of her self, a part of the person her prudence served. Besides, not all conflicts are worrisome. What made Hellman's so troubling? Perhaps she thought she had to do justice to all that she then cared about. In that case her issue was one of integrity, of being her full whole self. But could she have had (or been) a whole self before she put the parts together? And wasn't that just what she found so hard, to settle her conflict, to form a whole self?

2 IN OLD VIENNA

Not every difficult choice connects with a public political problem. There are narrowly personal issues that are as troubling as any. No one but you may care what you do, but often that makes it no easier.

A psychoanalysis is an engagement as personal as any can get. Should you invest the time and money? If the analysis is a success, it could reshape your life. If it fails, it could leave you worse off. Ought you to get involved? The issue was faced in the 1920s by the young Bruno Bettelheim, not yet an analyst himself or even planning to be one. In those days, in Freud's Vienna, the time investment was serious. A proper analysis meant six days a week, an hour a day, and it lasted for months.

There was no question of principle here. The question was about the results: Would they be worth what they cost? But what results could Bettelheim expect? And what would count as success? This last raised a special complication, for an analysis might affect his judgment. It might work a change in his values. It might turn him into a person whose values he wouldn't now approve but who then thought the change in himself had been a change for the good. Hellman writes that she told herself, "Just make sure you come out unashamed." She could have said, "Whatever happens, make sure that you keep your integrity." But what might later shame Bettelheim – or what he might then be glad he had done – depended on how he now chose. Can one demand integrity of oneself while arranging to make oneself over?

He consulted Richard Sterba, a well-regarded analyst, and asked whether he needed treatment. Sterba replied that he had no idea. He said he might know in a year or two, by which time Bettelheim would know that himself. Bettelheim asked whether analysis would help him. Again Sterba said that he didn't know, that only time would tell.

These answers left Bettelheim undecided. So he asked what point there was to going into analysis. What good could he expect from it? He reports that Sterba told him "that I would find the experience very interesting because I would discover things about myself that I had not known before. This would permit me to understand myself better and would make many aspects of my life and behavior more comprehensible to me."[2]

Bettelheim says that this settled it. Here was a man who didn't pretend, who didn't promise the moon, a man who could be trusted. But trust had not been the problem. The issue had been the costs and benefits: Was an analysis worth the trouble? And would an after-analysis approval of his analysis deserve any credence? This remained as open as ever, Sterba's remark having left it untouched. Indeed, that remark had been commonplace. It had said nothing that Bettelheim didn't know. How then did Bettelheim's doubts get lifted? Was there any logic to his reaction to being told what he knew all along?

We might have also asked these questions about how Hellman reacted to Fortas. How had Fortas helped her? How did his suggestion solve her problem? Her resistance to ratting remained, and so did her fear of jail. How then did the line he suggested get her to make up her mind? It may be that his calling it a "moral position" did the job for her, but why should these words have been so effective? How can a turn of phrase pull weight?

3 SOPHIE'S CHOICE

Here is a case very different, this one to chill the blood. The incident is fictional, but its sources are real enough.

William Styron's *Sophie's Choice* is set in New York in the late 1940s and speaks of the life of a troubled young woman. Sophie enters as an enigma; not until the end of the book is any light shed on it. We then learn that she was caught in a roundup in Nazi-occupied Poland and that she and her small son and daughter were shipped to the death camp at Auschwitz. There, on the entrance loading-ramp, the SS doctors made their "selections," deciding who was to go to the left, to the gas ovens, and who to the right, to the labor gangs. The doctor she faced was drunk, and the news that she wasn't Jewish provoked him to do her a favor:

> The doctor said, "You may keep one of your children."

Sophie didn't understand.

> "You may keep one of your children," he repeated. "The other one will have to go. Which one will you keep?"
>
> "You mean, I have to choose?"
>
> "You're a Polack, not a Yid. That gives you a privilege – a choice."
>
> Her thought processes dwindled, ceased. Then she felt her legs crumble. "I can't choose! I can't choose!" She began to scream . . . .
>
> The doctor was aware of unwanted attention. "Shut up!" he ordered. "Hurry now and choose. Choose, goddamnit, or I'll send them both over there. Quick!" . . .
>
> "Mama!" She heard Eva's thin but soaring cry at the instant that she thrust the child away from her . . . . "Take the baby!" she called out. "Take my little girl!"[3]

One reading of this ghoulish story is that the doctor got Sophie to join him. He made her an accomplice in the killing of her child. He got her to help with at least one "selection." But Styron also suggests something else, that the doctor failed with her, that she never did choose. Or rather, he leaves this matter dark. Her daughter cried out for attention, and Sophie, gripped by the cry, said "Take her!" Speaking these words wasn't choosing. What Sophie brought about, she didn't decide, she didn't *choose* to bring about. This would mean that she foiled the doctor, that she kept herself from him.

Sophie herself never saw it that way, and she never forgave herself. Perhaps there was more than she cared to report. Perhaps she recalled what she kept unspoken: her being suddenly drawn to her son, her being jolted by the girl's cry into the knowledge that she loved the boy more. In that case, perhaps she did choose. Perhaps – but did she or didn't she?

Sophie thrust the child forward. She had to act somehow, and so she did. But her action wasn't a choice, no more so than saying "Take her!" was. Here the reader may get uneasy. If an action isn't a choice, what *is* a choice? What is it to *choose*? We could have asked the same question before. When Hellman chose, what was it she did? At one moment, she was "bewildered"; at the next, her mind was made up. What happened in between? What happened was that she chose, and to choose is to make up one's mind. Yes, but what is the *making up* of a mind?

This question is light-years from Auschwitz. It may well seem far removed from any pressing issues of life. We want to talk about practical matters, about the real choices that trouble real people, and that may make for impatience here. When we consider how hard life can be, we may dismiss mere philosophy. Still, in a book, we are speaking of life; we are not trying to live it. We are standing off for a while, hoping to see how it all hangs together. In this book, we will look at our choices and at the reasons we have for them. We will speak of inner conflict and of risk and ambiguity, and we will ask what it means to choose rightly. But not much can be said about choosing unless we first say what choosing is. So we will start the next chapter with that.

2

HAVING REASONS

WE have to make choices, like it or not. And we often have a reason for the choice we are making. What is a choice? What is a reason? These are two basic questions here, and we need answers to them.

1 OPTIONS

Not just anything can be chosen. You can't choose to live forever. You can't choose to fly like a bird. This not because you can't in fact fly but because you don't think that you can. What you are choosing must be an option. It must be something you think you could do, something you think now up to you. Where you think nothing is up to you, you don't have any options. You are not facing an issue and don't have a choice to make.

First, about issues and options. A person has a choice to make – we will say that he faces an *issue* – only where he has options to choose from, and an *option* is (in part) an action he thinks up to him. In making a choice, we settle some issue. We fix on one of the options we have. And an option is an action we think we are free to take.

We think we are *free* to take an action where we think it is up to us, where we think we would take that action if we wanted to. Suppose that Hellman's situation were even worse than the one she reported – suppose that she had no money. She would then have faced no problem of choosing which lawyer to get to advise her. She could of course have made a list and asked herself who would be best. But she would have known from the start that no lawyer would take her case. Knowing that she wasn't free to get the person she picked from her list, she wouldn't have had any options. So there would have been nothing to choose.

Choices presuppose options, and having the option of doing something implies that you think you are free to do it. On a more usual way of speaking, it isn't your *thinking* you are free that counts but rather your *being* free. On this, your options needn't be actions you think you would take if you settled on them. They needn't be actions you think up to you. They are actions now up to you, whether or not you think they are. ("You can't choose love," the song says; the point may be that it's not up to you whether or not you fall in love, even if you think that it is.)

Let us avoid this second idea. The distinction between our being free and thinking we are free should matter. It should be possible to say of someone that he was free to do this or that but didn't know it and so couldn't choose. Also, that he chose to do it, thinking he was free, but wasn't.

Again, to choose, we must think we are free. Someone who thinks he is locked in a room has no choice about whether to leave. There is nothing for him to decide – even if that door in fact isn't locked. Also, what we choose to do, we needn't be free to do. We may choose from a restaurant menu only to learn that the kitchen is closed. We thought we could get the roast-chicken special; we *thought* that was up to us. Our being kept from getting that dinner doesn't mean that we didn't choose it.

Still, thinking that things are up to us doesn't suffice for choosing. Where we think that anything goes, we are not facing an issue. To choose, to have an issue to settle, we must admit certain limits. We must admit two sorts of constraints – call the first sort *only-one* constraints and the other *one-of-these* constraints.

We may have many options, but we must think we can take only one. Sometimes the *only-one* constraint is imposed by mere logic. We know we can't go both east and west. We know it has to be only one, and so, at some point, we have to choose. We know we can go both east and fast, so we don't have a choice to make there. Sometimes the constraints we are under are social. A person may have to choose between two possible careers, the current social realities allowing him only one. But most of us don't have to choose between a career and a marriage. We believe that we can have both, and so we don't face any issue in that.

There are also constraints of this sort that we impose on ourselves. Neither logic nor society rule out our overeating. We ourselves have ruled that out. We could have both the chicken and fish but for that rule we imposed on ourselves. With that rule in place, however, we now have to choose. People who let themselves eat as they please face no issue on such a matter; they have no choice to make.

We constrain ourselves further too: we want it to be *one of just these.* A chooser wants to make up his mind in some one of some set of ways, so he first has to shape that set. He must lay out the lines of action from which he will choose. Suppose you are thinking where to go in the summer and have it down to either England or France. Going to England and going to France are then your two options, and your choice must be one or the other. Going to Spain is not an option, and neither is jumping out of the window; you can't choose one of these. You can of course often start all over and expand the set of your options, but you can only choose in the end from the options you then have before you.

We have said that the agent must think of each of his options that he is free to take it, that he would take it if he wanted to. We must add that he doesn't yet want to take any particular one of them – that his mind is still *open.* Where his mind is made up on a subject, the issue is settled; there is nothing to choose.[1] Also, that he doesn't yet think of any option that he will take it or that he won't. Call this the *liveness* condition. If Hellman thought she would in the end cave in and appease the Committee, she wouldn't have had any issue beforehand of what to do when she went. Neither resisting nor not resisting would have been live options for her. Being sure of what she would do, she would have had no options left – or nothing we here will call *options.*

2 CHOOSING AS CHANGING

Let me pull this together. An issue is a set of options, and options are possible actions of which all the following holds. The agent doesn't yet want to take any particular one of these actions (this is the open-mind condition). He thinks of each of them that he would take it if he wanted to (the freedom condition). He thinks he can't take more than one (a constraint condition), and he wants to take one of just these (a second constraint condition). And he doesn't yet think of any that he will take it or that he won't (the liveness condition).

What is a choice – what is it to *choose*? I can now offer a simple answer. Where we have options, our mind is still open; we don't yet want this or that. To make a choice is to make up our mind, to settle some issue we face: to *choose* is to come to want to take this or that option we have.[2]

To choose is to come to want something that is an option for us. We may choose to have a good dinner or to see this or that movie. We then *want* to do these things, and we look forward to them. We may choose also to give up our job, to end a friendship, to get a divorce, and we then want to quit that job, to drop that friend, to leave our spouse. Wanting implies no eagerness here, no joyful looking-forward to it. So we must be careful not to read too much into wanting. We must try to think of wanting in a nonhedonic way, in a way that allows for our wanting what we know will be painful.

To choose is to come to want something, something that is an option for us. The second clause can't be left out, for not every coming-to-want is a choice. You get up in the morning, wanting your breakfast. You didn't want it when you went to bed, so at some point you *came to* want it. Still, you didn't then choose to have breakfast, this because you then faced no issue, no set of options of which breakfast was one. By contrast with this, you now raise an issue when you enter the kitchen. Will it be cereal? Will it be eggs? Will it just be coffee and toast? Your coming to want one of these will be choosing. So also where there is more at stake. Hellman faced the issue of what she would do before the Committee. Her coming to want to confront the Committee was the choice that she made.

But *is* a choice always a coming-to-want? You enter that kitchen and see the bread. That was bought last night. On the counter, you see the eggs – these have been there for years. You choose on the spot and start to make toast. But must you have *come to want* to do this? Isn't your choice just your *doing* it, your taking the action involved?

I am distinguishing choosing from acting, from acting *on* a choice. Often we choose before we act, in preparation for action. (Think of Hellman again.) And sometimes the action isn't then taken: we lose interest, or are hit by a truck, or are denied the occasion. (Say that Hellman made up her mind, but was then told that she needn't appear.) But whether or not we move into action, there was always a coming-to-want, at least where our mind was open before, for it then no longer is. And the change from open to closed – our coming-to-want this or that – was our choice.

Choosing is thus an inner changing, a coming-over to something new. Sometimes the change is trivial, as when we choose the toast. At other times, it isn't, which is why sometimes our choices matter whatever happens after we make them – why they sometimes matter to us whether or not we act on them. (How she had chosen would have mattered to Hellman even if the meeting were canceled.) Also why they sometimes matter to certain other people too.

Let us turn back to the doctor. The doctor ordered Sophie to choose. What made that order so monstrous? Her situation was awful enough; how did the order make it worse? Styron invents some biography. He suggests that, in his youth, the doctor had been religious, that he now again hungered for God, and that he hoped to awaken his faith by committing some "great sin." No doubt this is meant to sound false. It is meant to underscore the mystery of the doctor's malice. But how was he being malicious? What was he trying to do? How did his order provide for a "sin" going beyond all the rest?

He wanted Sophie to choose, to come to want this or that. He wanted her to come to want either her son's or her daughter's being killed. She cried out that she couldn't choose. She couldn't want a child of hers dead. He ordered her to want this, to change into someone who did, to become an accomplice to him, an inner killer of her child. Getting her to be such a killer was the sin that he had in mind.

Did the doctor achieve his purpose? Sophie pushed her daughter forward. She said, "Take my little girl!" These were just words and actions. I am saying that they don't count, that since she didn't want the child dead, she had not made a choice. On this view, she defeated the doctor, though she never realized it. She hadn't changed; she stayed as she was. She didn't grant him his sin.

3 BELIEFS AND DESIRES

Some choices we make have reasons behind them; others perhaps do not. What is a reason for making a choice? What is it to *have* a reason? There is an answer dating back to the Greeks, an incomplete answer but a promising one; it at least puts us on the right track. We will extend it in what follows. But first, the long-established idea, the classical theory of reasons.

On this theory, a reason is a mental state, a two-part mental state, one part a belief, the other a desire – a wanting of this or that. Suppose that someone chose to do *x*. He chose it for a reason if he thought x was of sort y (that it had the character or the likely consequence y) and he wanted to take some action of that general sort. This belief-and-desire compound was his reason for choosing x. We can (provisionally) also speak of it as his reason for *doing* x.[3]

We seldom lay out a reason this fully. We mention either the belief part only or only the desire part; no need to say more. Why did President Truman order the dropping of the atomic bomb? He wanted to hasten the end of the war. It goes without saying that he *believed* that dropping the bomb would do it. Why did President Ford pardon Nixon? He knew that that would put an end to a divisive public ordeal; no need to add that he *wanted* it ended. Still, a reason always consists of a belief and a related desire. If you think I am wrong about Truman, about why he dropped the bomb, you must think that some other belief-and-desire he had decided this for him. Pointing just to some different desire or purpose alone won't do (unless, again, the belief is then clear).

A person's reason for some choice and action brings about that choice and that action. The theory holds that reasons are causes, that our having a reason for something brings about that something – or rather, that it brings that about unless, having chosen, we change our mind or can't follow through or fail in the effort. I now have a reason for going up on the roof next Sunday, so I now decide to do it. On Sunday, I will get on that roof – unless I change my mind or break a leg or can't find a ladder. A reason can always be blocked or derailed, but as a rule we don't think that will happen. We expect a person's reasons to bring about what they are reasons for. That is what warrants our taking his reasons to explain what he does.

But here is a troubling scenario. Suppose that a rich old lady has died. Her niece is suspected of killing her, for she stood to inherit the money. The niece believed that killing her aunt would make her rich and she wanted to be rich. She had a suitable belief-and-desire, and so "she had a reason." The niece had a motive, or *grounds*. Suppose, however, the butler did it. The niece's motive didn't move her, and this though there was no change of mind or failure of effort or the like.

The niece's belief-and-desire (for money) didn't cause her to do the deed. It seems that it wasn't a full causal reason. Still, it was a belief-and-desire. Can we say it was somehow dormant, that it wasn't *active*, and that only *activated* beliefs-plus-desires give people reasons? Yes, we can (and we will say it), but that alone would not get us far. For what makes an active state active? What keeps the others *in*active? In the niece's situation, what switching-on factor was absent?

Was there something missing in the background of where she stood? Think of the butler, who did it. The butler believed that killing the aunt would enrich the niece and he wanted to enrich her; on the usual theory of reasons, that was the reason he had. This may look too simple. The butler, as a boy, had been brought up as a Mormon on very strict moral principles. He still accepted some of them. He knew the old lady was sleeping with the gardener, and this turned his mind against her. The butler's background set him up for what happened. It prepared him to do what he did. Nothing in the niece's background set her up to act in that way.

The background is frequently cited, what people do being traced to their childhood, to a strict or a slack education, often to poverty, to abuse, to bad parenting. Matters of that sort can't be ignored, but their bearing is indirect. The background at most predisposes. It can't account for who does what – why Jones, who was abused as a child, has become an abuser himself, while Smith has not, though he too was abused. It can't explain why Ford pardoned Nixon or why Truman dropped the bomb. And the whole point of the study of reasons is to provide us with explanations, to help us account for our choices and actions and for those of others.

Should we say that the missing factor is the intensity of the desire involved? Suppose that, aside from wanting the money, the niece wanted also to keep her hands clean. Suppose that she wanted her hands to be clean *more* than she wanted the money and that she thought one excluded the other. Should we say that someone who thinks that *x* is of sort *y* and wants to do something of that sort has a reason for *x*'ing only if there is nothing he wants as much (or more) that he thinks incompatible with it?

I don't think we should, for it won't always help, and we then are just where we were. Say that the niece wanted nothing as much as she wanted that money; still, she didn't act, and so our problem remains. In such cases, people speak sometimes of *weakness of will* (the will there weak though intense), but the phrase itself explains nothing. The question is, what held the niece back, what kept her will weak in this instance? Or rather, what was absent for her that, were it present, would have made her will strong?

Something is getting by us. Is that something eluding us because it is somehow unconscious? People aren't always aware of all that is currently moving them (or holding them back by its absence). True, but we have provided for that. We have not confined people's reasons to beliefs and desires of which they are conscious – to those they *know* that they have. The net we have cast is wide. Still, it is missing something.

4 THE MISSING FACTOR

We have mentioned child abuse. Is there a belief-and-desire reason that motivates a child abuser? We might ask too about rape: What moves some men to that? Every man wants sex and thinks that sufficient force might yield it, but most men aren't rapists. Beliefs and desires are not the whole story. What is being left out?

And again, about the niece who didn't kill her aunt. She had a belief-and-desire that gave her a "motive" to do it but she didn't. The butler believed and wanted the same, and he plunged ahead. How did their mind-sets differ? What was present for the butler that was absent for the niece?

To get a handle on this question, it may be best to look afield, at some far-out case. So let us return to that train ramp at Auschwitz and reflect on the doctors there. We needn't keep to Styron's fiction, for there is a historical record, including the transcripts of talks with these people after their capture (after the war). This has recently led to some useful psychological studies of them.[4]

The doctors were making "selections" – this was the word always used. That is, their job was to choose: this person to die, that one to live (if only until the next selection). The able-bodied were sent to work, the others were sent to be killed. The doctors "selecting" were in the SS, an ardently Nazi group. But though they had volunteered for the SS, they had not bargained on this. All of them protested when they first arrived. They asked for a transfer. They tried to get sick. A typical objection was that "selecting is not the province of a doctor . . . . [A doctor's] only purpose is to sustain life."[5] Still, almost all came over in the end.

The question is, what brought them over? The details differed from one to the other, but the basics were the same in each case. Their beliefs didn't change and neither did their values, what these people wanted to do and to help bring about. At least, their own later testimony argues against their beliefs or desires changing. Their minds were changed in another respect: they came to see things in a new light. They were brought to see selecting in a way that let them accept it. They were got to understand it so as to let them think it right.

Again, the details differed. Some doctors were reminded by the older hands that the Jews were "enemies of our race"; this let them see the selecting procedure as a part of the larger war. Others noted that killing these people spared them the brutality and squalor of the camp, the selections then seeming considerate, almost a sort of kindness. All were reminded they were SS officers, sworn to follow orders, and that the more painful their duty was, the more credit attached to their doing it. They came to see their selecting assignment as a burden they assumed for their cause. The euphemisms were helpful too: deciding on death was "ramp duty," genocide was the "Final Solution." These served to launder their first impressions. They helped to give them the understandings that let them do their part.

They had all known they were under orders and they all wanted to follow orders, but at first they saw the selecting not as an order but as malpractice, as a betrayal of medicine. They had also wanted to help to defeat the "enemies of our race," but in their state of shock on the ramp they had seen those people as *people.* The way they now saw things remedied that. Their new understandings connected the project to their Nazi "idealism," to their all-along values. Their understandings activated those beliefs and values; they made them apply to the case at hand. The doctors saw selecting then as what they had wanted to do all along. That summoned them to do it, and so their resistance lifted. "In the beginning it was almost impossible. Afterward it became almost routine."[6]

The doctors were facing a dreadful situation, and they reacted by changing their focus, by getting themselves to see their assignment as work that had to be done. They came to see it as something demanding, as something hard but manageable, as work they wanted to do. A great deal could be said about this, but let us just keep to our present business and speak of what it says about reasons. On that topic, the message is this, that reasons involve *understandings,* or (more loosely) *seeings,* that the full reason for what someone does includes his seeing it as something he wants to be doing.[7]

A person's understandings are a part of his reasons. They thus figure in every action that has some reason behind it. The doctors' case is special only because of the grisly horror of it. Also, the doctors had to find a new understanding of what they would do; the way they first saw things when they arrived had to be got around somehow. In more normal circumstances, the way people see things gives them no trouble. Thus we don't notice the role that it plays, and we don't often think about that.

Still, we have to think about it if we want to get clear about people. Take our question about the niece and the butler. Both believed that the death of the aunt would make the niece rich and both wanted her rich. But the niece didn't kill the old lady and the butler did; how come? I suggest that the answer is this, that the butler saw the killing as an enrichment of the niece but that the niece (it had crossed her mind!) saw it as murder, from which she backed off. The niece didn't see her killing her aunt as something she wanted to do. (It hadn't crossed her mind as an act of self-enrichment.) So her wanting to be rich never got connected for her. Her wanting the money wasn't called into play – her wanting it wasn't *activated.*

What about the rapist? The man who rapes and the man who doesn't are the same in their beliefs and desires. They both believe that a show of force might frighten some woman into having sex with them, and they both want sex. They differ in their understandings. The rapist sees rape as raw, rough sex, as tough-guy sex, the way he likes it. The other sees rape as a violation. He wants sex, but not violation, and so the way he understands rape doesn't connect with what he wants, which means that he isn't moved to rape. Here too, how the action is seen is decisive. (Though sometimes the case may be this instead: the rapist also sees rape as a violation, and he *wants* to violate.)

The rapist is one step from the child abuser, or from the sort of child abuser who sees his having sex with children as easy, trouble-free (one-way) sex – again, the way he likes it. We may think that understanding weird, but weirdness needn't surprise us. (Was seeing genocide as a "solution" not weird, seeing it as a sort of achievement?) Besides, a person's beliefs and desires can be very peculiar too. A person's reasons are not the less reasons for being odd or foolish or weird. And my point is that how he sees things plays a role in his reasons.

How he sees things also figures in what counts as a choice he makes. Here we have to refine our initial analysis of choosing. The doctors had wanted all along to do whatever their duty was. They also wanted to help to root out the so-called inferior races, etc. They chose in the end to participate, but they didn't only then *come to want* to participate. They had wanted to do that all along under various descriptions of it, none of them fixing on how they saw it when they were face to face with it. So we can't say that to choose is to come to want one of our options. We have to say that to choose is to come to want it *as we understand it.*

This calls for some related refinements of our concepts of freedom and options. We must say now about freedom to act that we are free to take an action where we would take it if we wanted to take it *as we understood it.* We must say about our options that we want to take one of just these *as in the end we will understand it* and that we don't yet want to take any *as we understand it now.* (The doctors' options were selecting and refusing. They saw selecting at first as malpractice, and they backed off from that – they didn't want to engage in malpractice. They saw refusing then as rebellion, and they backed off from that too.)

There are now two kinds of choices. In one kind, the threshold change is a change in what the agent wants; in the other, it is a change in how he understands some option. In one, the understanding precedes the new wanting: the agent comes to want to do something as he understood it before. (The butler had perhaps always seen what he might do as an enrichment of the niece but only came to want to enrich her after he fell in love with her.) In the other, the wanting comes first, the agent coming to see some option as the sort of action he already wants to take. (The doctors came to see selecting as their duty, which they always wanted to do.) Here the agent makes his choice in coming to have the new understanding; he doesn't come to want what he hadn't wanted in some way before. Still, he newly comes to want-it-as-he-(newly)-understands-it. So the idea that choosing something is coming to want it *as we understand it* covers both kinds of choices.

5 THREE-PART REASONS

A person's understandings play a role in his reasons. This means we have to expand our initial, two-dimensional concept of reasons. We must fit in the agent's understandings as a separate factor, letting a reason be a structured, *three*-part mental state. Suppose that someone chose to do *x*. He chose it for a reason if he thought *x* was of sort *y* and he wanted to take some action of that general sort – *and* he understood *x* in terms of *y*. This belief-plus-desire-plus-understanding is here the reason this person had. The theory remains that reasons are causes, that having a reason brings about what then follows (provided the person doesn't change his mind or break a leg or die), but this has to be read in terms of our three-part concept of reasons.[8]

Still, we now must touch it up slightly. The reason we have for making some choice is also our reason for acting it out, but it isn't always the reason for whatever we then do. Sometimes, in taking action *x*, we are acting unwittingly. Say that we have a reason for pressing a certain button – it is a doorbell button. It happens that, in pressing that button, we detonate a bomb. Whatever caused the button pressing caused the detonation, but though we pressed that button for a reason, we had no reason for setting off the bomb. We wanted to do what we did, but only as a button pressing, not as a bomb detonation. And we can only have a reason for doing what we want to do *as we understand it*. So, yes, our reason for choosing *x* is also our reason for acting it out, but only under the description of it that figured in our reason for the choice.[9]

Once more to the case of the butler. The butler *thought* that killing the lady would enrich the niece, he *wanted* to enrich her, and he *saw* the whole business that way – as an enrichment of the niece. This belief and desire and understanding together were his reason for deciding to do it (as also for his then doing it, as he understood it). Again, we seldom need to lay out a person's reason in this much detail; one factor often points to the others. The butler's wanting to make the niece rich says all that needs to be said.

Let us keep the concept of *grounds* we introduced a few pages back. This has two parts only: a person has grounds for what he is doing where he has certain beliefs and desires. Grounds alone aren't reasons. The niece believed that killing her aunt would make her rich and she wanted to be rich, but in her view the killing was murder, and that connected with nothing she wanted. So she had grounds for killing the lady, but seeing the action as she then saw it, she had no reason for doing it – no full causal reason. (A roundabout way of putting this: a person's grounds are a possible reason minus the understanding part.)

A person can have a reason for doing what he believes would bring about *y* though there is something else he wants more and thinks incompatible with it. That is, our wanting *y* may figure in our reason for *x*'ing though we want some *z* more than *y* and think we can't have both. Perhaps the niece indeed wanted the money more than she wanted clean hands. She had a reason nonetheless for doing nothing to get it, for she thought that doing nothing would keep her hands clean and she wanted them clean – *and* she saw inaction here as keeping her hands clean.

The niece was weak willed regarding the money. Though she wanted to have that money and wanted nothing else more, she was not moved to reach for it. Our new theory accounts for such weakness. It holds that our will is weak regarding some *y* that we want where we want *y* only under descriptions that don't express how we see it. Our will is weak regarding *y* where it isn't enlivened by our understanding, isn't *activated* by it – where we have grounds for reaching for *y* but don't have a full reason. The niece was eager for the money – she wanted to get to be rich – but she saw her enrichment as murder and so that desire lacked force. Seeing her getting rich as she did, she lacked a full reason for taking any action.[10]

The concept of seeings, of understandings, is the central concept here. How might that be defined? *What* we understand are actions and events and situations – I will use the word "facts" as a catchall – and our understandings are our conceivings and labelings of the facts understood. They are the mental *hold* we have on them, our *prehension* of them. The selfsame fact can be differently understood, but at any single moment we can't understand it in more than one way (though that way may be compound, a thus-*and*-so way of seeing, the conjuncts there being our *partial* understandings).[11]

This does not define the concept, or at least not usefully, nor can I offer a better definition. I think that the concept can't be defined in any noncircular way, that it is too basic a concept to be spelled out in terms of others. Beliefs and desires are equally basic, and equally undefinable. But we don't always need definitions. We can often make do with examples, letting these show how our concepts apply.

What needs most to be stressed is this, that understandings aren't beliefs. The understanding you have of something as its being of a certain sort isn't the same as your believing that it is of that sort. True, the two states are related, for the understanding implies the belief. The butler's seeing his killing the aunt as an enrichment of the niece implies that he believed the niece would be enriched. Still, the seeing and the belief were distinct mental states. The butler might have had that belief and not have had that understanding; he might have seen the killing differently, perhaps as moral retribution (the aunt's affair with the gardener!). What is believed about some fact constrains how that fact can be understood. It doesn't reveal how it *is* understood.

Another example: a marathon runner. The runner knows that the race he just ran took him much longer than it took the winner. He knows too that it took him today five minutes less than it took him last year, that today he beat his own record. Still, he may see it in one of these ways – he may dwell on just that aspect, brooding on it or rejoicing over it – and not see it now the other way. One more example: a person at thirty. If he thinks his life is half over, he must think he has half his life left. But he may see that selfsame fact in one of these ways and not in the other. He must *believe* he has half his life left, but he needn't also have that upbeat understanding of it.

No single instance can give us a handle on the concept of understandings, but enough instances of various sorts (the doctors, the butler, the rapist, the runner) will give us all we need. Some more strictly visual matters might be mentioned too: the picture of the Necker cube that can be seen facing this way or that, the drawing that can be seen as that of a duck or that of a rabbit, the Rohrschach inkblot that can be seen in totally different ways. Our topic here is the seeing of actions and events, not that of objects, like pictures. Still, *someone's drawing a certain picture* counts as a kind of action, and that can be seen as his drawing a duck-picture or as his drawing a rabbit-picture. So these cases are like the above, or at least closely related, and they too may help to turn us toward the idea of understandings.[12]

We can also approach the idea from yet another direction, by noting that we can't account for all our dealings with people without it. Think of the various ways in which we try to change people's minds, our own as well as others'. The butler decided to go ahead, but perhaps only after some thought. Perhaps he had to convince himself first that the niece would benefit. He wanted to enrich the niece, but where were the riches to come from? Not until he was convinced that the niece was in the aunt's will did he decide to act.

To *convince* someone is to change his beliefs, to get him to believe what he didn't before. That is one kind of changeover. Sometimes the change we hope to arrange is not in the other's beliefs. He lacks some desire we want him to have and we try to instill that desire. We try to get him to want what he doesn't – we try to *induce* him to want it. Let the niece be as we said: wanting to be rich, but backing off from murder. Let her, however, have no objection to the butler's doing it. If he is neutral to her being rich, if her enrichment is nothing he wants, she might try to induce him to want it. She might offer to share the wealth. Or she might play on his love for her, telling him that *she* wants it.

She might also try something else. She might try to get him to see the killing as an act of mercy (the aunt is very sick). Or she might try to get him to see it as an enrichment of himself (she reminds him that she would share), or as a proof of his love. In such cases, we speak of *persuasion,* a changing not of beliefs or desires but of someone's understanding of something.

This is certainly common enough, but let us keep here to vivid scenes. We spoke of the Nazi doctors being persuaded to see selecting as a duty. In a case from longer ago, Macbeth resisted killing the king. He knew that, if he killed him today, he would himself be king tomorrow, and he wanted badly to be king. But he saw the killing as a betrayal, and that held him back. He said,

> He's here in double trust.
> First, as I am his kinsman and his subject,
> Strong both against the deed; then, as his host,
> Who should against his murderer shut the door,
> Not bear the knife myself.

Killing would betray a trust, a trust imposed twice over. He refused to stoop to that.

Lady Macbeth didn't argue with the facts; of course killing would be betrayal. Macbeth's beliefs were not at issue, and neither was what he wanted. She argued that he was *seeing* things wrong, that his understanding was shameful, that his voice was that of fear. Since he wanted so much to be king, going ahead would be *manliness.* It would be the *bold* thing to do. Backing off would be *cowardice:*

> Art thou afeard to be the same in thine own act and valour
> As thou art in desire? Wouldst thou . . .
> Live a coward in thine own esteem . . . ?[13]

She knew how he valued boldness. That is why she pressed just this.

Macbeth defended his view of the matter. Yes, of course, the act would be bold. But it was she who was seeing it wrong: it would be a *betrayal.* Still, in the end she persuaded him. He came to see it as she wanted him to, and that brought him over.

Or take the cases in Chapter 1. Sterba got Bettelheim to enter analysis by telling him it would help him to know himself better. We asked how that could have worked; surely it wasn't news. It worked not by adding to Bettelheim's beliefs but by changing his focus on things, by changing his perspective. He had been thinking about an analysis in terms of his current emotional problems. Sterba suggested, take a different perspective. Don't think in such local terms only. Think of what you might learn: see analysis as an education. Bettelheim reports being taken by that. Here was a breath of fresh air – life would at least become interesting! What Sterba said had been trite, but sometimes a trite remark isn't pointless. It tells us nothing we didn't know, but if it gives us a new understanding, it may still ring a bell for us.

Likewise with Fortas and Hellman. Here too was a kind of persuasion, though here in the context of Fortas's proposing a new course of action. He could have called that a middle course, which wouldn't have done much for Hellman. Instead, he called it a "moral position," and Hellman was glad to find an option that counted as moral and yet wasn't reckless. Its being "moral" dispelled her anxiety about betraying her principles and that settled things for her.[14]

My use of "convince," "induce," and "persuade" may be thought a bit strained. Still, I am only using these words to distinguish three sorts of operations – three sorts of influencing, of changing someone's mind. And the point of that is to stress the distinctness of three sorts of mental states, the sorts of states these operations affect: beliefs, desires, and understandings. Convincing and persuading are different operations, whatever labels we put on them. And they are only different because understandings are not beliefs, because how a person sees things can change even where all his beliefs stay the same.[15]

A final remark about understandings. I have spoken of seeing something in these terms or in those. Must understandings be in some *terms* – must they always be *in words*? Can't there be wordless (ineffable) understandings? We needn't express some understanding we have; it may, in that sense, be wordless. But I assume that understandings are expressible, that we *could* put our own into words. Or that others could do that for us – this allowing for the inarticulate, and even for infants' and animals' understandings. The "terms" in which we see some fact are thus the terms in which our understanding could be put. Still, nothing here hinges on wordability.

6 EMOTIONS AND EXCUSES

A grab bag of questions and topics remains. First, we have considered the roles of beliefs and desires and understandings only. Does nothing else figure in motivation? Don't the emotions we have play a part? What about love and hate? What about envy, ambition, and pride? Our emotions stir us to act. Don't they enter our reasons?

Yes, they sometimes do; but then they just are desires we have, desires of a special, insistent sort. An ambition is a desire for some worldly advancement. An envy is a desire for another's possessions, or for that other person's looks or style or wit or whatever. No problem with such emotions. They enter our reasons directly as their desire components. (On the usual reading of Macbeth, he was prompted by ambition and was brought to see the murder as a way of satisfying *that*.)

Other emotions enter our reasons only indirectly. They enter sometimes by determining what we want. A man in love with a woman wants to see her, to touch her, to be intimate with her. Also, he wants to make her happy and perhaps rich (remember the butler). If he hates someone, he wants him to squirm or to hurt or to suffer – if you hate a number of people, you may want something different for each. Sometimes too, emotions enter by shaping people's understandings. (The butler's love for the niece got him to think in terms of enriching her.) So love and hate and the like also enter, but only at a remove, by way of the desires and understandings that they call forth in us.

How does a single emotion (say, love) make for so much variety? This question is as open as ever. Still, it isn't about people's reasons, about what their reasons are like. It is about how people get the reasons that they have. I said above that love and hate enter our reasons indirectly. Better perhaps, they don't enter at all but play a part in shaping what does.

A question of a different sort: Why do we want to know our own reasons? What good is our knowing our reasons to us? We have already noted the answer. We want to make sense of ourselves; we want to account for what we are doing and for what we did. Yes, but why in terms of our reasons? Why not instead in terms of physics or of neuroscience? Because these can't explain what we do as we see it (or saw it when we did it). They can't explain it in a way that brings out how it was our own doing, how it reflected our self at the time (as we see that self). Explanations in terms of our reasons account for our conduct, so understood, and thus they do the job we want done. What about somebody else's reasons; why should the reasons that move a person be of interest to others? The answer is much the same. A person's reasons help others too to make sense of that person, to explain what he did. And sometimes also to predict his behavior – and to guard against it.

No need to expand on this here.[16] It may be better to pause to consider what people's reasons don't do for them. A reason serves to explain. It doesn't suffice for a justification: a person's having had a reason doesn't *justify* what he did. Truman certainly had a reason for ordering the bombing of Hiroshima. What should he later have thought of his order? What ought people today to think of it? Recalling the reason that Truman had isn't enough to answer these questions.

Nor do reasons always exonerate where something wrong was done. They don't all *excuse* the agent, though some people think that they do. A reason, they note, is always a cause, and whatever is caused has to happen – it *must.* Perhaps the agent was free to act otherwise before he had his reason in place; but once that was set, he wasn't. No point then in blaming this person. He was only the passive medium for certain forces of nature.

This would let Macbeth be excused, and also the butler and the doctors too, and most of us would resist that. These people can be called to account *because* of the reasons they had. Not only do reasons often not excuse; often (as here) they stand against that – they exclude exoneration. Better for people if their minds weren't on it, if they had no reason at all, or if the reason that moved them to act was a reason for doing something different. They could then say they didn't know they were doing it, that they wanted to do something else. Though often that doesn't wash either. We tell them that they *should* have known, or that it doesn't matter what they wanted. (Reasons don't always exonerate, and often the absence of a reason doesn't either.)

But doesn't an action's having been caused mean that we weren't free when we took it? The question here is that of free will, of determinism versus freedom of action. I incline to the answer presented in the philosophy of David Hume. Hume's idea has two parts. First, he defines our being free as compatible with determinism. All events are determined, those in which we are agents included, for every event is caused. But where we are agents, the actions we take are sometimes caused by our reasons for them, and that, Hume says, is what marks us as free. Hume's definition comes to this: a person is acting freely where he is acting "according to the determinations" of his reasons.

This improves on my initial statement about what it means to be free, that a person is free to do something where he would do it *if he wanted to.*[17] Hume considers a person free where he would do it *if he had a reason,* his concept of people's reasons being of the usual two-factor sort. Put in our new three-factor terms, the general idea still is this, that we are free to take some action where we would take it if we had a reason. Also, that we are acting freely where we are acting on our reasons. Our actions then (as we see them) are ours in that they derive from ourselves. This means that our reasons can't be excuses. Since it is our reasons for them that keep us from disowning our actions, it is just our having those reasons that makes us responsible for them.

Still, aren't our reasons caused too? If so, one might say, we *must* have those reasons, and why be blamed for what we couldn't avoid? Hume's second point addresses this. Hume says that we find no *must*ness in nature. Causation is a matter of regularity only, not of any constraint. It has to with with what follows what, with sequences, not with pushes and shoves – in Hume's terms, with *conjunction,* not with *compulsion:* "Beyond the constant *conjunction* of similar objects and the consequent inference from one to the other, we have no notion of any necessity of connection." So our reasons having been caused doesn't imply that we had to have them. We might have avoided having those reasons. We might have had reasons for doing something else. And so again, no excuses.[18]

There remains the question of the reasons we *ought* to have had, of whether our reasons were good ones. If things turned out badly but we had a good reason, we might then have an excuse. A plea just of good intentions won't clear us; we can't just say what we wanted was right. But a good *reason* might help. (Some people believe Truman's reason was a good one.) Still, what is a good reason? Let us put that question off.

3

RATIONALITY

PEOPLE are said to be rational animals. Better, perhaps, we *can* be rational, and we often are. When are we rational and when not? What counts as being rational? What counts as a rational *choice*? This chapter reports the consensus on this and also some open issues.

1 CERTAINTY

Rational people look ahead. They look to the outcomes of what they might do, to what they might bring about. And they reach for what they think would come out the best for them. Where you are rational, you want to do what, all considered, offers you most, and you choose an option you think is of that sort.

Here is a case of the simplest kind. You have to fly to Paris tonight, and the only seats you can get are on American and on Air France. The planes will leave at about the same time, and their flight times are much the same too. They offer the same sort of services, and you think that both are safe (no hijackers, no bombs). You learn that the fare on American is lower. That settles it for you: American it is.

In such simple situations, you know exactly what to expect. You are certain of the outcome (fare paying included) of each of your options, and you rank the outcomes in some clear order of preference. The choices you make in such situations are said to be *under certainty,* and their logic is obvious. A rational person wants to do what would come out best for him. Where he is choosing under certainty, he thus wants to take an option to whose outcome he prefers that of no other – to whose outcome, as he understands it, he prefers no other outcome, as he understands the others. And he chooses an option he thinks is of that sort.

I may seem to be conflating two distinct ideas here. A rational person chooses what he thinks will have the best outcome, and he follows his preferences, whatever they happen to be. These would indeed be different ideas if bestness were something objective, if it were some objective measure of the benefits to be had. But I am thinking here of bestness in a subjective sense: what is best is what stands highest in the agent's own ranking. An outcome here is best for a person if he prefers none other to it (as he understands them all).[1] So these aren't two different ideas but just two ways of putting the same.

Must there always be a best outcome? The answer has to be *no,* for sometimes a person is inconsistent. Perhaps he prefers one outcome to a second, the second to a third, and the third to the first. Where these are the only outcomes, there is then no best; each is bested by some other. Let us sidestep this complication by assuming that the agent is consistent, or that at least there are no cycles in his preference ranking.[2]

What if there are several options whose outcomes are ranked together as best? Think of the famous story of the donkey standing between two bales of hay. The donkey was hungry, but the two bales looked alike. Neither appealed to him more than the other. Being indifferent between the outcomes of going right and of going left, the donkey moved toward neither bale and starved in the midst of plenty.

Had that donkey been rational, he would not have starved. A rational agent chooses an option whose outcome he thinks would be best for him, an option he cannot improve on. If he thinks there are several such, he chooses any one of them, it doesn't matter which. Were the donkey rational, he might have tossed a coin. He could have let that govern his choice and then acted on that.[3]

On the concept presented here, what makes a choice rational

are the agent's *grounds*, not the reasons he has. A rational person wants to take a certain sort of option, an option whose outcome is best for him. And he chooses one of the options he believes is of that sort. This belief-and-desire of his isn't what moves him to choose. It isn't this person's reason – a reason is a belief-and-desire-plus-understanding. Again, the belief and desire alone are the agent's *grounds*. And a choice someone makes is rational where he has grounds of the best-outcome sort for it.

A choice can have one reason only, but it can have many grounds. We can have grounds for the choices we make that are not part of the reasons that move us. Think of a student applying to college. He may choose to attend a certain school because he knows it is far from home and he wants to be far from home and he sees his being there as his being far from home. That is then the reason he has, and it says nothing about what is best. Still, it may be he wants the best and that he thinks this school would be best – perhaps he has this too in mind, though it isn't a part of what moves him. If he does, he has rational grounds, and his choice is rational.

His choice is then rational, though his reason isn't. We can say that *reasons* are rational where their component beliefs and desires constitute grounds for rational choices, and we might now look for a word for choices deriving from rational reasons. But we won't be needing this concept – the one we have will do. That speaks of rational *grounding* only: the choices we make are rational where we have *grounds* of a certain sort for them. They are no less rational where those grounds aren't part of our reasons (where our reasons aren't rational too).

2 RISK

Certainty is hard to come by. Most of the time, we make do with less. Sometimes we aren't sure what would follow if we did this or that but know only what *might* follow; we know different outcomes that are possible. Suppose we can say of each of the outcomes of each of our options how likely it is – how *probable* it is – and also how much it offers us. We are then facing what is called a choice problem *under risk,* and for such problems a special logic exists.

This logic dates back to the seventeenth century, its central concept of probability itself not going back much further.[4] It was first applied to various sorts of intricate gambling problems. Should a person accept a certain bet? How much is this or that gamble worth? Here is one of the classical problems. Two dice will be tossed 24 times, and you will get $60 if a double six appears at least once. What is this gamble worth to you?

The basic idea was this. Each possible outcome of taking an option (in an issue of the betting type) offers the agent some monetary benefit. The worth of an option (in such an issue) is its *expected* benefit, the weighted average of the benefits of its outcomes, the weights being the probabilities of the outcomes that would provide them. And a rational person chooses an option that maximizes his expected benefit.

Think of the betting problem cited. You are offered $60 with the probability x – the probability of at least one double six in 24 tosses of two dice – and would get nothing with the probability y, that is, $1 - x$. On the expected benefit idea, the worth of the gamble is x times $60 plus y times $0. Since x is .4914,[5] this comes to $29.48, and a rational bettor would refuse to pay more than that.

In the gamble, the possible benefits were getting $60 and getting nothing. The English word "benefit" derives from the Latin for "the good thing done" – one such good thing might be getting $60, and the early theory of risk looked at the monetary goods (and bads). The modern theory abstracts from this. It distinguishes the benefit itself, the good thing done, from the goodness of it, its goodness to the agent, its value to him in his own estimation. Getting $60 is a good thing. Its goodness or value to the agent came to be called the *utility* he sets on it.

The modern concept applies very broadly. We can speak of

the utility a person sets on his getting some money. We can speak too of the utility he sets on his writing a poem, on his eating some hay, on his moving far from home, on someone else's moving, even on some benefit (or harm) he might do to some other person. Here goodness, or utility, is like bestness above. It isn't a measure of objective worth but of subjective valuation. The utility that someone sets on something measures how much he wants it, how much he prefers it to other things.

The early theory spoke of the benefits to be had; the modern theory speaks of utilities instead. It speaks of the utilities of the possible outcomes and of the *expected* utility of the option whose outcomes they would be. This last is the probability-weighted average of the utilities the agent sets on these outcomes – the probability-weighted average of his present valuations of them.[6] And we can put the logic like this, that a rational person wants to take an option that maximizes his expected utility, an option than which no other option has a greater such expectation, and that he chooses an option he thinks is of that sort.

Some critics think this is too demanding. In their view, a rational person isn't always a maximizer. It often is foolish to try for the most: it is counterproductive. If we wait for the highest bid, we may wind up losing business. If we wait till we find the best move, we may forfeit the game. A rational person sets his sights lower. He aims at what is good enough, at what would *satisfy* him. He doesn't maximize; he *satisfices.*

This faults the benefit theory, not the one we now have. Granted, a rational person doesn't always reach for the biggest benefit (the biggest profit, steak, or drink). He doesn't always reach for the biggest because he expects to do better if he doesn't. (Often a smaller drink would be better.) And he wants the most, the best: he is trying to maximize. There is no paradox here. A rational person is often content to satisfice his expected benefit because he is a maximizer of expected *utility* – of the weighted average of the utilities of the outcomes.[7]

A person may sometimes have several options that maximize

expected utility, and the theory we now have lets him choose any one of them. Some critics think this too lax. They insist there are in such cases other matters that should be considered. Where some options are tied at the top, they hold that these options must be looked at more closely.

Different ideas have been proposed regarding what should be looked for in them, but only that of *maximining* has had any serious run. Suppose that several of your options maximize expected utility. For each of your top-tied options, notice what would be the worst it could lead to. Then choose that option (or one of the several) whose worst possible outcome is no worse than that of any other. That is, choose an option whose worst or *minimal* outcome is the best or *maximal* of the different worst possibles. In brief, choose an option that maximizes the minimum – choose an option that *maximins.* (Several options may maximin, but then you could look to their next-to-worst outcomes and repeat the procedure – this is called *leximining.*)

An option's worst-possible outcome is said to mark its *security level:* if you take this option, you can't get less than that. An option's *best*-possible outcome marks what is called its *hope limit:* the agent can't hope for more.[8] The question now is this. Where your expected utilities leave certain options tied at the top, will you, if you are rational, attend to security and choose by maximining? Or will you attend to what you might hope and *maximax* instead, choosing an option (or one of the several) than which no other has a better *best*-possible outcome? Or will you reject these refinements and not look beyond expectedness?

Consider your betting problem again. The gamble offers you an x-probability of getting \$60 and a y-probability of getting nothing. So its expected utility is x times the utility of getting \$60 plus y times the utility of getting nothing.[9] Let there be some sum of money, M, such that the utility of getting M is just equal to that expected utility, and say that accepting the gamble and accepting M are your only options. The maximin theory looks to security, and so it calls for choosing M – it says that a rational person will refuse to gamble in such a case. The maximax theory looks to hope limits, so it calls for choosing the gamble. The basic theory, unrefined, holds that either choice would be rational. I will keep to the basic theory, but nothing in what follows depends on not going beyond it.

3 MORE ABOUT RISK

The maximizing-utility logic of risk is often called *Bayesian* (after Thomas Bayes, an eighteenth-century writer). It applies neatly in dicing problems having to do with small sums of money. In these, there are commonly accepted ways of finding the probabilities involved and the utilities can be put in terms of the money to be gained or lost. Very few problems that people face are of this clear-cut sort. Still, the Bayesian logic assumes precise numerical utilities and probabilities. Is that at all realistic? Do people in typical, real-life situations assign utilities and probabilities?

Bayesianism has to say *yes*, which flies in the face of the obvious. But an ingenious analysis by the economist Frank Ramsey shows how a yes answer might be defended.[10] Or rather, it shows what comes close to this, that people whose preferences have best and worst items and are suitably consistent and plentiful always assign numerical utilities and probabilities. They may be unaware they are doing this; most of them *are* unaware of it. But their preferences, all together, imply precise utility and probability assignments and, in that sense, these people *make* them.

Ramsey's analysis has been shaped and revised and restated in various ways.[11] The details of this are more than we need, but here is the basic idea. Suppose that the agent prefers some prospect to every other (say, peace and good will all around) and that there is another prospect to which he prefers every other (say, the whole planet destroyed). Assign any pair of numbers to these best and worst items – let it be 100 and 0.

Ramsey shows how to find a prospect the agent ranks midway in value between them – give that the utility-value 50 – and how to find items ranked midway between that and the endpoints – these get valued at 75 and 25 – and then how to find still further items ranked midway between all these, etc. This forms a dense spectrum of prospects, each item in it having a numerical utility fixed by the numbers we gave the extremes. Every prospect or possible situation is now either in this spectrum or ranked on a par with some item in it. So either the utility of a prospect or situation is set by the midway-placing procedure or its utility is that of the item with which the agent ranks it.

This gives us numerical utilities – a numerical scaling of value, and Ramsey shows how probabilities follow if we assume some consistency.[12] Bayesian theory thus gets what it needs. Still, we may be uneasy, for this measurement of values is weak; it isn't like that of, say, weight. If one rock weighs 75 pounds and another weighs 25, the first is three times as heavy as the second. The same can't be said about utilities: a prospect x we value at 75 isn't three times as valuable to us as some prospect y we value at 25. The fact that the number we assign to x is three times the number we assign to y only reflects our having set the extremes of the scale at 100 and 0. If we had initially valued the extremes at 100 and −100, we would now value x and y at 50 and −50, and the ratio would no longer be 3.

The numbers do tell us something. The measurement of utility here is like the usual measurement of temperature, which depends on an initial setting of numbers on the boiling point and the freezing point of water. In neither case can we speak of ratios, but in both we can say that some item is half or a third or a fourth of the way from this point to that. Normal body temperature is 37% of the way from the freezing to the boiling points of water, whatever the scale. The utility of x in the paragraph above is $\frac{3}{4}$ of the way from the worst to the best – again, whatever the scale. In the accepted terminology, neither temperatures nor utilities are *ratio* measurable but both are *interval* measurable. (Probabilities *are* ratio measurable.)

There remains an important difference between the cases of utility and of temperature. No problem with determining temperatures; for that, we have the thermometer. We have nothing like a thermometer to help us to find the utilities we assign. If our preferences mark best and worst items and are suitably consistent and plentiful, it follows that we assign utilities and probabilities to every possible situation. The utilities and probabilities are implicit in our preferences; this much we get from Ramsey. Still, what *are* those utilities and probabilities? We can sometimes (in certain gambles) assume that the utilities appear in the money outcomes and the probabilities in the objective chances. But the issues we commonly face provide for no such assumptions. (The outcomes aren't sums of money and the chances aren't known.)

Does that mean that the Bayesian theory has to fail us in practice? The reader will have to decide. This can be said in its favor, that it tells us how certain factors combine to specify what would be rational for us. It tells us to think in terms of the utilities and probabilities we assign in a case, to look for the option that has the greatest *expected* utility. It doesn't show us how to establish particular expected utilities, but we don't always need to do that. For instance, say that option x has just two possible outcomes. Say that these are the same as the possible outcomes of y but that the more desirable outcome is more likely if x is taken than if y is. Here we know that x has a greater expected utility than y though we cannot tell what either expected utility is.

This too can be said for this theory, that it lets us do without a separate logic for certainty. Think of problems under certainty as those special problems under risk in which some outcome of each of our options has the probability 1. The Bayesian logic of risk then gives us our logic of certainty as a bonus. So we don't need two logics here; a single logic will serve.

4 AMBIGUITY

Certainty is the simplest case, and risk is a departure from that. Consider now a different sort of problems departing from certainty. Say that, whatever the agent might do, he is sure of what would follow, that he knows of each of his options what the outcome of his taking it would be. But suppose he has several rankings of these different outcomes, different rankings from different points of view. This person is facing ambiguity. He has no unambiguous ranking of the outcomes he foresees, or at least he ranks no outcome unambiguously highest.

Let us revise our initial problem of choosing a flight to Paris. You have to take either American or Air France, and again, the fare on American is lower. But the Air France flight now leaves at a time more convenient for you. Also, the American flight is shorter but the Air France food is better. Here you must somehow consider all this and take it all into account.

Or suppose you are buying a car and have brought the issue down to getting either a Honda or a Volvo. Whichever you buy, the outcome is clear: you will own the car that you bought. Still, thinking of cost, you prefer having the Honda, but, thinking of safety, you prefer having the Volvo. The Honda is the more easy to maintain; the Volvo is the more comfortable, etc. Neither outcome is better than the other from each point of view – neither is better in every dimension. Here too you have several rankings of the outcomes and must somehow combine them. You must combine each outcome's utilities in its different aspects.

The plane and the car scenarios are instances of what is called *multidimensional* choosing – or sometimes, multi*attribute* or multi*objective* choosing. We will say they are instances of problems of choosing *under ambiguity.* A person awake to the complexity of situations (to their ambiguity) often faces such problems.[13] In our simple plane and car cases, he knows what the outcome of each option would be, so no probabilities enter. The logic he needs is not that of risk, but it is very similar. For here too, facing ambiguity, he may be able to work out an average. The value of each of the options he has (of buying a Honda, buying a Volvo) appears then in the weighted average of the utilities he sets on its outcome in its different aspects (cost, safety, comfort, etc.), the weights now being the *importance* to him of these dimensions or aspects, their importance relative to each other. The logic of choice under ambiguity is like that for problems under risk except that, in place of expected utilities, we here have *importance*-weighted averages.

This assumes we can measure the relative importance to us of different dimensions. Is this assumption plausible? The Ramsey method of measuring utilities can't be adapted for the measurement of importance, for that method looks to our preferences, and dimensions aren't prospects, the sort of items we have preferences over. We prefer owning a car that is safe to owning a car that cost us a lot (these are two different prospects), but we don't prefer safety to cost. Besides, Ramsey provides just for interval measurement, and the logic here proposed requires importance to be ratio-measurable. It requires us to be able to say that some dimension is three or four times as important to us as another.[14]

Perhaps we might find some way of scaling each separate dimension – the dimension itself, not its importance to us. (Safety is sometimes scaled in terms of the number of accidents per 10,000 miles driven.) And perhaps we could then determine our trade-off rates for the different dimensions and let that measure their relative importance. How much safety would we give up for, say, each unit of savings in cost? Could we answer this in a way that is independent of the separate scalings and independent also of the levels (of cost and safety) from which the trade-offs are made? If not, is there some other way of ratio-measuring the importance of dimensions? The logic of ambiguity proposed depends on the answer to this being *yes*. But the issue is certainly open.[15]

If the reader is uneasy with this, he can adopt a less all-at-once logic. He can say that a person facing ambiguity thinks in terms of priorities, in terms of first things first. (Safety perhaps comes first for him, nothing else counting on that first level.) Such a person still reflects on the utilities he sets on the outcomes under their different dimensions, but he does that sequentially, in what is called a *lexical* (or *lexicographical*) way. He averages first among the dimensions having the top priority for him – straight averaging here, no weight assignments, no ratio-measurement of importance. If just one option comes out best, that settles it for him: he chooses that option. If several options are tied as best, he turns to the dimension that has the next priority, etc. (He first seeks out the safest car, since he lets nothing count against safety. If several cars are equally safest, he considers their cost, etc.) This makes do without ratio-measurement but it may often look blinkered and foolish. (Must we always buy the safest car? What if that car is only marginally safer than the next safest but costs ten times more?)

Let us pass lexicality by and return to our basic logic. That is, let us take the measurability of dimension- or aspect-importance for granted. Thus far, all has been neat and clear; risk hasn't entered the picture. In the messier cases, the agent faces ambiguity and he also faces risk, and he must cope with both together. He has to choose from among his options unsure of what their outcomes would be – this gives him a problem under risk. And he must do that while setting different utilities on the possible outcomes under their different aspects – this makes it an ambiguity problem.

Suppose you have two job offers and aren't sure about either job. The outcomes will depend on how the economy goes (this is the risky part). And besides, however that goes, your valuations of the outcomes differ under their different aspects (this is the ambiguity part). You prefer more money to less, and you prefer the bigger challenge, but the job that offers more money would challenge you less than the lower-paying job. Here you will have to average twice. First you will have to put summary values on each of the possible outcomes. That will require averaging your different valuations under income and challenge, this in a way that reflects the relative importance of these factors to you. Then, on the basis of that being done, you will have to sum up again, averaging then for both of your options in a way that reflects the probabilities of their different possible outcomes – the outcome if the economy improves, if it stays flat, if it worsens.

The logic of choice under ambiguity connects with a topic we met in Chapter 1. We spoke there of people being concerned that their actions don't leave them ashamed, that their choices and actions issue from their total selves, that they retain their integrity. This may well have been Hellman's concern when she appeared before the Committee and perhaps also Bettelheim's when he first thought of analysis. Integrity doubtless means many things, but a concern for one's total self implies an attention to all that matters, a suitably balanced or *weighted* attention. We express such a weighted attention where we choose among our options in the light of the importance to us of their different aspects (or of the different aspects of their outcomes). Hellman's options stacked up one way under prudence and another way under principle, but importance-weighting these factors let her make up her mind. Still, that misses the difficult part. We will have to say more about this, and we will also have to consider Bettelheim's problem of integrating over time.

5 VAGUENESS

The problem for Bettelheim wasn't only that his values might change, that he might change his values himself by how he now chose and acted. What troubled him at least as much was that he had to choose in the dark. Was it likely that an analysis would take him out of the slump he was in? How probable was it to make things worse? How probable was it that nothing would happen, that he would just be wasting his time? Not only did Bettelheim not have the answers, he didn't think there *were* any answers, or any that were clear and precise. He saw no precise probabilities he might have taken into account.

Think of Hellman's problem too. Did we do justice to that? Was the problem she had a problem under ambiguity only? She was intent on integrating the two conflicting concerns that she had, on balancing prudence against principle. But we suggested this meant she had to weigh them in terms of their importance to her, their relative importance (relative to each other), and she would have said that she couldn't. It was a central part of her problem that such a weighing wasn't possible, that at least it wasn't possible in any precise and clear-cut manner, that the relative importance of prudence and principle couldn't be neatly fixed.

Bettelheim and Hellman were facing problems of a very common sort, problems that are often described as being under *un*certainty. These problems are not under certainty; to that extent, the usual label is proper. But let us here speak of them instead as problems under *vagueness*. The special, distinguishing mark of these problems is a lack of precision. Sometimes the agent can't assign precise probabilities or utilities. Sometimes he can't assign precise importance weights to the different aspects of the outcomes. And where there is any sort of vagueness, he can't compute a weighted average.

A follower of Ramsey dismisses such cases. He thinks of them as marginal only. He holds that Ramsey's analysis shows that vagueness exists just for mental slouches, that a consistent person always has fully precise probabilities and utilities, and he might add that it suggests that consistency calls for precise importance weights too.[16] A person who is consistent often (typically!) doesn't know his own mind. He can't report the subjective specifics. He can't *identify* his probabilities, etc., but they are there, under the wraps, and he must guess at them somehow.

Where someone says he is facing vagueness, he is admitting to inconsistency (or is refusing to guess).

Ramsey's analysis hangs together, but it depends on his adopting a stringent consistency concept. This concept requires that every prospect or situation not in the best-to-worst spectrum be ranked on a par with some item in it, and with one such only – the last bit ensuring that every prospect is assigned a single, precise utility. If *x* and *z* are in the spectrum, *x* preferred to *z*, then *y* can't be set on a par with *x* and also with *z*. Parity here is indifference, the absence of preference either way, and so Ramsey needs consistency to require the transitivity of indifference: if you are indifferent between *x* and *y* (if you prefer neither to the other) and also between *y* and *z*, you must also, to be consistent, be indifferent between *x* and *z*.

Again, Ramsey needs this principle; without it he can't establish that people always have precise probabilities and utilities, though some of them only under wraps. That is, without it, he can't rule out vagueness. So if we departed from Ramsey and had consistency *not* implying this principle, vagueness would be possible even for people who are fully consistent. Suppose that *x* is preferred to *z* and that *y* is set on a par with *x* and also with *z* and also with every item ranked between *x* and *z* (and with no other). Indifference (parity) isn't transitive here. And we might say that the utility of *y* isn't point-precise, that it spreads out vaguely between the utilities of *x* and of *z*.[17]

But can it be right to dismiss the principle of the transitivity of indifference? Let *x* be a halibut-with-capers dinner, *y* a haddock dinner, and *z* a halibut-with-lemon-sauce dinner. Are you inconsistent if you are indifferent between *x* and *y* and also between *y* and *z* but not between *x* and *z*? (You dislike every sort of fish, disliking all fish equally, but prefer capers to lemon.) I don't think you ought to be faulted; and if you can't be faulted for it, you can't be said to be inconsistent. So I think we should allow for indifferences not being transitive. This provides for vagueness, and that brings up the question of the logic of choosing under vagueness.

There is much disagreement on this. Various logics have been proposed, but none has firmly established itself. For instance, the logic of maximining: where you must choose under vagueness, choose an option whose worst possible outcome is no worse than that of any other.[18] Maximaxing has come up too, though perhaps for contrast only: choose an option whose *best* possible outcome is as good as the best outcome of any other. Both these ideas have to do only with probability or importance-weight vagueness. Both assume that the utilities of the outcomes (which is best and which worst) are precise.

A third idea expands on the fact that vagueness is a matter of degree. Utilities and probabilities (and importance weights too) can be more or less vague – totally vague, or very vague, or just a little, or not at all. Vagueness thus occupies ranges. The utility of an outcome might be precisely *m*. No vagueness there whatever. Or it might range from *m* to *n*, which could be the extremes of the utility scale – that would mean total vagueness – or any two points in between, the further apart the greater the vagueness. And so too for probabilities (and for importance weights).

Every option now comports with one or many expected utilities (and their importance-weight analogues). Or rather, each option *has* one or more, *one* where there is no vagueness at all, *many* where there is some vagueness. In the former situation, we get the case of risk (or ambiguity), and there the usual logic applies. In the latter, every selection of utilities and probabilities from the ranges involved – every constriction of the ranges to points – cuts the *many* down to *one*.[19] Every such selection determines a unique expected utility for each option, and we can here generalize our basic maximizing logic. We can speak of choosing an option whose expected utility, on some selection from the ranges, is at least as great as that of any other, on the same selection. We can say that a rational person wants to take such an option and that he chooses one that he thinks is of that sort.[20]

We will speak of such an option as a *rationalizable* option. That lets us put it this way, that a rational person choosing under vagueness chooses some option he thinks rationalizable. Again, this only generalizes our logic of risk (and ambiguity). But the idea may seem too contrived, so we won't pursue it.

6 INTENSIONALITY

Suppose you arrive at a concert, having bought a ticket beforehand, and cannot find your ticket. However you lost it, the ticket is gone. It cost you $20. You must decide: Will you buy another, or will you just go home?

Here is a second scenario. You didn't buy your ticket beforehand, but put the money aside for it in your pocket. When you get to the box office, your pocket is empty – in this situation, your *money* is gone. Will you buy a ticket anyway (you have some money in your other pocket), or will you now go home?

It appears that many people would buy in the second case but not in the first. Can any sense be made of that? In both situations, they can either buy a ticket and hear the concert or not buy a ticket and go home. Since the outcomes both of buying and of not buying are the same in these situations, what sense does it make to decide one way in one and the other way in the other?

Or think of the uproar some years ago when gas stations first allowed credit-card payments. Some stations added a markup to the price for those who used their cards, which led some card users to boycott those stations. The stations then canceled the markup, raised the price for everyone, and offered a discount to those who paid cash, which put an end to the boycott. There were people who didn't use cards during the markup period who were willing to use them later when they would have got a discount if they paid in cash. What sense can be made of these people? Can we account for their reasoning?

Such questions come up repeatedly in the work of Daniel Kahneman and Amos Tversky, who have run many experiments on what are called *preference reversals* – we will, more broadly, call them *value* reversals. In a value-reversal story, people are presented two times over with what in fact is the same issue, though that issue is presented to them differently the two times. The first time they face it, they decide one way; the second time, some contrary way.

Here is a typical Kahneman and Tversky experiment.[21] The subjects were put in two situations. Each person in Situation I was told to assume he had just gotten 1,000 (in the local currency). He was then asked to choose between (*A*) getting another 500 for sure and (*B*) an even chance of getting another 1,000 or getting nothing more. In Situation II, each subject was told to assume that he had been given *2,000* and was asked to choose between (*C*) *losing* 500 and (*D*) an even chance of losing 1,000 or losing nothing. The majority of the people in I chose *A*, and the majority of those in II chose *D*. If they had been in both situations (first in one and then the other), many might have chosen both *A* and *D*.

Would choosing *A* and *D* make sense? Kahneman and Tversky think of it this way. Getting 1,000 and then 500 more comes to the same as getting 2,000 and then losing 500 – either way, one has 1,500. And getting 1,000 and then an even chance of getting another 1,000 or getting nothing more comes to the same as getting 2,000 and then an even chance of losing 1,000 or losing nothing. So Situations I and II reduce to the same. In each, the agents chose between winding up with 1,500 and an even chance of winding up with 2,000 or with 1,000. Those in both I and II thus would have faced the same issue twice. And many would have chosen one option the first time and turned it down the second time, choosing the other then instead.

The authors preface their report of this experiment by saying,

"We now show how choices may be altered by varying the representation of outcomes."[22] They would account for our other two cases in a similar manner. In the gas station case, people first heard they must pay either the regular price *x* in cash or the marked-up price *y* and then that they could pay either the discounted price *x* in cash or the regular price *y*. Either way, it was either *x* or *y*, but some people chose *x* in one context and chose *y* in the other. Likewise in the concert case. In both of the concert scenarios, people could either buy a ticket and hear the concert or not buy and turn back, and many took the first option in one (having come to *want* to take it) and the second in the other. The message is that people are sensitive to how a situation is reported to them, that their values (here, what they want) can be "reversed" by different descriptions of the same facts.[23]

Such reversals may strike some readers as a mark of soft-headedness. They may say that value reversers attend too much to the descriptions of things, that they neglect the objective reality (the objective sameness) of the situations described. Kahneman and Tversky would agree. They consider it a basic condition of a person's being rational that his choices *not* be sensitive to the descriptions he accepts of situations, to how he understands the facts involved, to how those facts are "framed"[24] – they call this the principle of *invariance*. Others label it *extensionality*. The contrary of this is *intensionality*, and that is often said to mark a person as *not* being rational.[25]

I reject this judgment of what is rational and what is not. We let a person's choices be sensitive to his beliefs and desires, and we assign a role to his subjective utilities and probabilities. Why then chafe at the thought of letting his understandings play a role too? I have shown how rationality allows our understandings a role – outcomes enter our thinking about them only as we understand them. And (in Chapter 2) I argued that our understandings shape our reasons. Let us pause to look back now and note how that bears on the cases here.

First, about our reasons. I argued that the reasons we have reflect how we see our options, that one part of every reason is some grasp of the action it backs. The way we see what we might do connects it with these or those of our values, and different ways of seeing an action connect it with different values. Chapter 2 showed us the doctors resisting selecting when they saw it as malpractice and then, later, getting involved when they saw it as ethnic cleansing: they had, from the start, endorsed ethnic cleansing, though they opposed malpractice. It showed us Macbeth resisting the murder when he saw it as a betrayal and eager for it and lunging ahead when he saw it as boldness: he was disposed all along to boldness, though he despised betrayal. Our seeings enlist certain values we have, different seeings tapping different values, and the values so tapped or enlisted enter the reasons that move us.

Our options connect with what we want by way of how we see them – by way of our understandings of them. And so too, reversing this, the values we have connect with our options via our understandings. Most of our values on any occasion don't connect with the issues we face, and their being unconnected keeps those values nonfunctional there. Think of Macbeth again. Macbeth despised betrayal even as he thrust the knife. The values that earlier kept him from this hadn't been rejected. Rather, the change in his understandings disconnected those values. And, in the process, it wired up others. We have been speaking of value reversal; we might now speak of value *disconnection* and of value *rewiring.* (We spoke before of value *activation,* another word for the same.)

It seems to me likely that the credit-card users can be explained along the same lines. The new description of the gas station policy changed their understandings. What they had seen as inviting a penalty (having to pay for using their cards) they came to see as turning down an incentive (the discount they would get if they didn't). This change rewired their circuits, disconnecting their opposition to being unfairly penalized and connecting their willingness to reject a nuisance incentive. They drove in one day for gas, intending to pay in cash, adopted the incentives point of view, and wound up using a card. In the initial wiring context, they had a reason for paying in cash. In their newly rewired state, they had a reason for using their cards. Both what they had intended to do and what in the end they did had a reason.

The concert-ticket case is similar (though we must be careful here about what we count as reversals). This case has to do with sunk costs, with money already spent on a project and gone whatever now follows. People who keep their sunk costs in mind report a ticket purchase in the two situations differently. In the first, $20 has been spent, and money that is spent is sunk. Since these people count it, however, they would, if they bought another ticket, see their total outlay as $40. In the second, the total outlay would be only $20 (the money lost hadn't been *spent*, it hadn't gone *for a ticket*). A purchase is seen in one situation as just the buying of a $20 ticket and in the other as the completion of an investment of $40 – too much money for a concert! These people are keeping track of what preceded, which affects their understandings of their options. And that enlists different values they have, giving them a reason to buy in one situation and not the other. If bygones had been bygones for them, their understandings would have been different, and that would have wired up different values and given them a reason to act differently.

Likewise with the *A*-and-*D* choosers in the Kahneman and Tversky experiment.[26] Here we have to speak of sunk gains rather than of sunk costs – or perhaps better, of *locked-in* gains, of benefits collected. Say that these people saw the money they got at the start as safely locked in. Say that they considered the outcomes from a baseline of *now* – that, unlike the concert goers, they put the past out of mind. Their expected gains and losses were then different in Situations I and II. Option *A* offered a gain of 500 and option *C* a loss of 500. And if we suppose, as

Kahneman and Tversky do, that they were risk averse for gains and risk inclined for losses,[27] they valued the outcome of *B* (a gamble on gains) at *less* than a gain of 500 and that of *D* (a gamble on losses) at *more* than a loss of 500. So they valued *A* above *B* and *D* above *C*, as they saw these options. This gave them their reasons for choosing as they did.

Say they had been like the concert goers (those who didn't replace their lost tickets) and started their bookkeeping further back – say that they measured the outcomes from a baseline *before* they got the 1,000 or 2,000. Their gains and expected gains (as they would have counted them then) would have been the same in I and in II, and there would have been no losses. All of the outcomes being gains or gambles on possible gains, there would have been no risk inclination in either situation. So *A* would still have ranked above *B*, but *C* would now have ranked above *D*, and that would have made for reasons for choosing *A* and *C* (not *A* and *D*).[28]

My concept of reversals is Kahneman and Tversky's, though I should say that I apply it here differently. They hold that the options in I and II are exactly the same, and that the options in the two concert situations are the same too, that what differs is only how the options are described. But this can't be correct. Either you are in one situation or you are in the other: either you just got 1,000 or you just got 2,000, either you lost your ticket or your money. And options in different situations are different; not all in one option is also in the other. What we have here are different descriptions of different options certain people have. That can't make for value reversals.[29]

Still, each of the different options involved might be differently described. In both their scenarios, the concert goers might or might not bring their sunk costs into their descriptions of their options. So too, the people in the experiment might or might not look to sunk gains both in I and in II. For each of the options involved, these people could measure the outcomes from a baseline in the past (before they bought that ticket they lost, before they got the 1,000 or 2,000) or from a baseline of *now* – and then follow suit in their descriptions of the options themselves. Their shifting from one to the other understanding (from one to the other baseline) would enlist different values they have, and so a shift from one to the other would make for value reversals. In the experiment, we find no reversals as we look from I to II. To find reversals, we must suppose that the *A*-and-*D* choosers had in fact shifted (from a back-then to a now baseline) and then compare the choices they made to the ones that they *would* have made if they had not made that shift.

The sensitivity of people's choices to how they see things can be explained. It squares with the idea that a person's reasons take in his understandings; it is, in that sense, reasonable. The last case also helps us to show how it accords with being rational too. Our choice of a certain option is rational if we have rational grounds for that choice, and we have such grounds if we want to choose an option with the best possible outcome and we think that what we are choosing is of just that sort. How we understand our options plays no role in this. Still, how we understand their outcomes bears on which options qualify.

Look at the *A*-and-*D* choosers again, and suppose they were risk averse for gains and risk inclined for losses. If they understood the outcomes as we have been supposing they did (exclusive of sunk gains), the outcome of *A* was best in I for them, as they understood that outcome, and that of *D* best in II. Assuming also that they knew this and wanted to choose what had the best outcome, these people had rational grounds for choosing *A* in I and *D* in II. If they had seen the outcomes instead in terms of their total assets in them (including the sums handed out at the start), *A* and *C* would have had the best outcomes, as these outcomes would have been seen, and this would have made for rational grounds for choosing *A* and *C;* a choice of *D* would *not* have been rational. So choices that are rational in one context of understandings needn't be rational in another.

Here we collide with a prejudice we noted in passing above.

This holds that rational choices always must be *extensional,* that they can't be sensitive to how the chooser understands the facts – call this Principle *R.* Our choice of a certain option is rational only if we expect the most from it, and I am saying that whether we do may depend on how we see its outcome and the outcomes of the others. We may value an outcome differently under different descriptions of it, but by fixing on this one or that, our understandings determine (select) which of our values count. If our understandings change, the values that count may thus change too, and that may affect how we rank the outcomes and so may determine which outcomes are best. It follows that, counter to Principle *R,* how a person might rationally choose *may* depend on his understandings of the outcomes.

This supposes that we sometimes value an outcome differently under different descriptions, even if we believe that the outcome described is the same. The critic responds that, where we do that, we depart from logic from the start. He offers us Principle *S,* which rules out certain combinations of values and beliefs. On this second extensionality principle, if you believe that *x* and *y* report the same fact (same event or situation), the values you set can't differ: you have to value the fact qua *x* the same as you value that fact qua *y.* How you *understand* that fact – whether you see it as *x* or as *y* – cannot make any difference.

Principle *S* is a principle of the consistency of beliefs and values. It refers to possible junctures of a person's mental states, to people's holding these or those values when they hold *those* beliefs. And the people in our stories certainly went against it. Macbeth set very different values on the killing qua betrayal and the killing qua boldness, though he knew it was the same action. The credit-card users valued the markup one way qua penalty and another way qua disincentive. So too with the people in the concert case and in the sunk-gains experiment. All these people went against the new principle.

So much the worse for the principle. In all the above, I reject it, finding no reason to hold myself to it.[30] I reject Principle *S*, though of course I must accept this – call it Principle *T* – that if *x* and *y* are the same *object of valuation*, they must be valued the same.[31] Principle *T* is trivial: on whatever you put some value, you must put that value. Does this mean that the same events or situations must be valued the same? No, for these don't get valued at all – not directly, not *simpliciter.* We value what happens as it is *reported*, as we or as others *present* it. Again: a killing, a homicide. This gets either condemned or excused as murder or as self-defense, as betrayal or tyrannicide – as however the act is described. We judge it not in its nakedness, but as clothed in this way or that. (Putting the point more traditionally, our values are not *de re* but *de dicto*.)[32]

T and *S* should not be confused. *T* says that, if they are the same value object, *x* and *y* must be valued the same. *S* says that, even if they aren't the same, we must value them the same if we think they report the same fact. *T* has no bite, but *S* is demanding; and again, the people we spoke of (Macbeth and the others) did violate *S*. I am saying that they needn't be faulted, that we needn't require values to be extensional in the sense of *S*. Our logic here is *in*tensional. It does not impose *S*.

There may remain some uneasiness. Say that you know that *x* and *y* report the selfsame option. And suppose too that, counter to *S*, you want to take that option qua *x* and *not* to take it qua *y*. (You want to rebuff the Committee but also *not* to risk jail.) You are here in a conflict. Rejecting *S* allows for confliction; it lets our conflicts accord with logic. Can we accept a logic so lax? We take up that question in Chapter 4.

4

SHAPING UP

NONE of us has his house in good order. We live in an inner disarray, in a jumble of beliefs and desires. Sometimes that makes for conflicts, setting up divisions inside. We will now look at some of the ways in which we can be divided. And we will see how we cope with that, how we manage to reason and choose in spite of being divided.

1 CONFLICTS

The title of one of Kierkegaard's books is *Purity of Heart Is to Will One Thing*. Kierkegaard was obsessed with God, and this book of his is a sermon, but the idea expressed in its title resonates beyond religion.

It has been put in various ways. In place of a vision of purity, an image of wholeness often is offered. The talk is then of *wholeness* of heart: *whole-heartedness* is to will just one thing. Sometimes not the heart but the mind is the part we are urged to keep whole. Kierkegaard quotes the apostle James, who spoke against being "double-minded."[1] There it is *oneness* or *single-mindedness* that is pressed on the reader.

Kierkegaard spoke of what people *will*. We might speak instead of what *matters* to us, of what it is we *care about*. No problem where only one thing matters; we will of course there go for that. The question is, what if many things matter? There is a character in a TV series who reports herself always as being *unanimous*. A fortunate woman – she is always whole-hearted.

But how about the rest of us, who are not always unanimous inside?

Think about Hellman again. When she considered her principles (not bringing trouble on others, etc.), she inclined to rebuff the Committee. When she considered what prudence advised (avoiding jail), she held herself back. Hellman's principles mattered to her, but being prudent mattered too. She didn't care about just one thing. How did this raise a problem for her, and how are such problems dealt with?

Let us return to basics, to *wanting* to act in this way or that. A failure of wholeness sometimes appears in an inner conflict of wants, and that may explain the concern people have about their not being whole. Conflicts are said to disable, to inhibit both choosing and acting.

This overshoots the mark. Hellman wanted to keep to her principles. She also wanted to do what was prudent. And she knew that principled conduct was in her case *im*prudent. Let us call this special sort of situation a *conflict.* A conflict is a distinctive structure of desires and a belief: the agent wants *x* and also wants *y* (each under a certain description), and he believes that he can't have both. We will be speaking only of conflicts in which *x* and *y* are *options,* the only options the agent has.[2] Hellman was in such a conflict, yet she chose and she acted.

Conflicts don't always disable, but the self-inhibition remains, a kind of self-frustration. Where we are involved in a conflict, we expect to deny ourselves something. We expect to have to say *no* to something that we want. So we try to get around this; we try to resolve the conflict. And if it turns out we can't resolve it, we try to soften the harshness of that. We try to arrange to have a reason for this or that we might do, and thus a way of making sense of denying ourselves what conflicts with it.

This gives us two initial points. The first is that a person can choose and act though his conflicts are unresolved. The conflicts he has needn't hold him down; they allow him to move ahead.[3] The second is that a person in conflict can find a reason for what he will do; a conflict allows for *reasoned* conduct. Hellman not only wasn't disabled, she managed to settle her mind. She settled her conflict, though she didn't resolve it.

We can pass the first point by; the second point concerns us here more. It brings out two senses of ending a conflict, of that conflict's lifting. A conflict might be *resolved*. In such a case, the agent pulls back; he ceases to want either *x* or *y* or to think that he can't have both. That happens where he reconsiders, or learns a bit more, or the situation changes (and he then learns that it changed). Where a conflict he has is resolved, he thinks he can have all he wants. So he is in the clear.

Sometimes there is no pulling back. The wantings and beliefs involved are dug in. The conflict then can't be resolved. Some writers find in this a basic fact about the human condition. They hold that it means that, sometimes at least, we cannot act for what we think best. Because of the conflict we are then in, nothing is uncontestedly best. What is best from one perspective comes out worse from another.[4] Perhaps indeed, going still further, "Every decision in this life is wrong from some point of view."[5]

Yes, perhaps, but not a real worry. Perhaps some conflicts can't be resolved. They might yet be *settled*, and a conflict that is settled is no longer disturbing. Where the agent has settled his conflict, he must still deny himself something, but he can make his peace with that. For he has found a reason for taking just this option or just that one. He remains conflicted, but his course is clear to him. It is still wrong from some points of view, but it isn't from his.

2 SETTLING THEM

Let us draw still another distinction, this one between two sorts of conflicts, two sorts of unsettled conflicts – call them *ambivalences* and *quandaries*. Both a person who is ambivalent and a person in a quandary are in an inner conflict. Both want *x* and also want *y* and think these can't be had together. The difference in their situations has to do with their understandings, with how they see or fail to see their options *x* and *y*.

We have quoted Hellman as saying that she found herself "bewildered," and we reported this in terms of our concept of ambiguity. We supposed that she saw her options from two different perspectives together and that this inclined her to acting in what she knew were opposite ways. From the point of view of principle, she wanted *x*, to rebuff the Committee. From the point of view of prudence, she wanted *y*, to do what they asked. (Here *x* is rebuffing qua principled action and *y* is appeasing qua prudence.) But she saw each option she had in both these ways together, one option as principled and imprudent, the other as prudent and unprincipled, and she had no ranking of them in terms of all she saw in them. So she was left with contrary promptings and with no way to adjudicate that. A person in such a situation can be described as *ambivalent*.

Ambivalence has to do with ambiguity, but a person facing ambiguity needn't be ambivalent. Think of the car-buyer's problem again.[6] Ambivalence is a sort of conflict, and a person buying a car and looking both to safety and to cost needn't have a conflict. He considers both safety and cost, but he needn't want to buy the safest and also the cheapest car. Hellman's case was different. She wanted to take the principled course and also to take the prudent one, which meant that she *was* in a conflict. She saw her options in both ways together, and so she was facing ambiguity. That made her conflict an ambivalence.

There is also a second construal of what Hellman called her "bewilderment." From the point view of principle, she wanted *x*; from that of prudence, *y*. But she didn't now see her options from both perspectives together, nor could she keep to either for long. Moving from one to the other, she had no hold on the options she had, no understanding (in our sense) of them. She "didn't know what to think" of them, what to "care about" in them, and that is why she dithered. On this second reading of her, she didn't face ambiguity here, but rather a kind of anxious blur. She was in a *quandary.*

We often can't tell which sort of a conflict a person before us is in, but that person himself will seldom be in doubt. He knows his own understandings as well as he knows his beliefs and desires, and whether he is in an ambivalence or a quandary depends on those understandings. Does it make any difference to him whether his conflict is of this sort or that? Yes, it does; for which sort it is determines how he might settle it.

An ambivalent person sees his options partly in one way and partly in another, and his different (part-)perspectives make for the conflict he has. Some sort of pulling together is needed, some summary valuation of his options as he sees them from all his perspectives together. The logic of choosing under ambiguity suggests that he weigh the different perspectives in terms of their relative importance to him and let the so-weighted average valuations of his options be their all-in-all values. This would establish a summary ranking of his options qua all he sees in them. Say he now has formed such a ranking and that one option stands higher than the other.[7] And suppose that he wants to take the option that here stands the higher, that he knows which option that is, and that he sees it as the one standing higher. He then has a reason for choosing and taking that higher-ranked option (and none for choosing the other). His conflict has been settled.

Does settling a conflict resolve it? Sometimes yes, sometimes no. Where our newly formed all-in-all ranking leads us to stop wanting this or that option, the conflict we had is resolved. Our initial desires and beliefs are then thought of as only first run (only "prima facie"), and we give up these or those if they don't square with our final reasons. But there are also other cases in which in the end we give up nothing. We then want all we wanted before and still think we can't have it all – we are still not "single-minded." Our conflict isn't resolved. Nonetheless, it has been settled and it no longer disturbs us. Such a conflict might be called *silent.*

This has to do with ambivalence conflicts. Where the agent is in a quandary he must proceed very differently. His problem is not that he sees his options in a number of ways together. Rather, he sees the options he has in no suitable way at all. He has no fixed understandings of them, or none in the terms of what he wants; he vacillates or draws a blank. Here he must try to focus himself, to fix on some way of seeing some option that connects it with something he wants to be doing. The conflict he has may then be resolved or may remain (as a silent conflict). He will, however, be out of his quandary, for he will have directed himself to just one of his options. His conflict will be settled.

Take the case of Hamlet; or rather, take Ernest Jones's classic Freudian study of Hamlet.[8] Hamlet's issue was whether (and when) to kill Claudius, his uncle. He knew that his father had been murdered by Claudius, and he wanted to avenge his father. But he also was deeply troubled by thoughts of his mother, Gertrude. That lady was Claudius's sister-in-law, and it drove Hamlet wild to think that Claudius was sleeping with her, a union then counting as incest. Hamlet was in a conflict here because he too lusted for Gertrude. He wanted *not* to punish incest, for that would have called for his facing himself. And yet he knew he couldn't fully avenge his father without punishing incest.

What made Hamlet's conflict a quandary was that he found no suitable understanding of either his killing or his not-killing Claudius. The ones that connected with what he wanted wouldn't stay put in his mind. He couldn't think in terms of avenging the murder of his father, this because he couldn't see Claudius in the role of a murderer; the image of him in bed with Gertrude kept getting in the way. Nor could he think in terms of punishing Claudius's doings with Gertrude, for he wanted to do the same, and all the less could let himself think in terms of punishing incest. Things finally fell into place for him when Gertrude drank the poison. Claudius's doings with Gertrude had then led to her death, and the shock and horror of that got Hamlet to focus his mind. He then saw his killing Claudius as avenging multiple crimes ("Here, thou incestuous, murderous, damned Dane . . ."), and that gave him his reason to act. Hamlet's conflict wasn't resolved. He still wanted all he wanted before. But it was over: it was *settled.*

Another possible reading of Hamlet's quandary is this. Hamlet wanted to avenge his father, but he also wanted to avoid getting his mother all to himself, for he dreaded what that would involve. And he knew it was one or the other; if he avenged his father, he alone would have his mother. With Gertrude dead, no conflict remained. Hamlet's conflict here was *resolved,* for he now could avenge his father without being left with his mother.

Neither of these readings is Jones's own. He proposes a third, an ego/id sort of analysis. On this reading, Hamlet still (unconsciously) wanted to sleep with his mother, but he resisted that desire, wanting (this unconsciously too) to be rid of his wanting her. He struggled against that, he tried to reject it, but his effort failed. Here is a kind of self-opposition different from that of conflict.

In a conflict, a person wants two things he thinks he can't have together. Here he wants something and wants *not to want it:* he wants not to want what he wants. His inner division is vertical, two desires on different levels opposing each other here. This could be called an inner *struggle* or an inner *dissonance.* Our discussion of people's conflicts carries over to struggles, though what we said about the settling of conflicts may here not apply. Inner struggles seem to end only where they have been resolved, one of the dissonant wantings being then given up. Hamlet's struggle (if that's what it was) ended when Gertrude died, for he stopped wanting her then.

A person's higher-level wantings sometimes are called his

will, and his being locked in a struggle is said to reveal a weakness of his will. (Here the concepts of will and of weakness are different from those in Chapter 2.) As long as a person's struggle persists, his will isn't getting its way with him. It can't undo his lower-level desires – these might be called his *inclinations*. On Jones's theory, there was no conflict; there was instead an inner struggle, and Hamlet's will was weak. It couldn't unseat his inclinations. He wanted his mother though he wanted not to want her. His weakness put him into a bind until, at the end, her death set him free.[9]

There is at least the possibility of conflicts of still another sort, of conflicts that aren't ambivalences and aren't quandaries either. If Hellman had seen rebuffing as principled (and not also as being imprudent) and appeasing as just prudent (not also as being unprincipled), she would have had a reason for taking whichever course she took. Since she inclined to both of them and knew that it had to be one or the other, she would have been in a conflict. This would have been an unsettled conflict, though she wouldn't have lacked any reasons. She would have had *too many* reasons: countervailing reasons. Call such a conflict an *overload*.[10]

Are there in fact any overload conflicts? I am assuming that there are not, for our having countervailing reasons would mean that reasons couldn't always be causes. Still, this new challenge could be met. It would just call for more qualification. We said at the start that reasons are causes only where the agent doesn't change his mind or break a leg or the like. We could now add that reasons are causes only in the absence of countervailing reasons.

3 UNITY THROUGH TIME

If you are rational, you go by the outcomes, by what you think would follow. Often you know that what would follow wouldn't follow all at once. You know it would come in a stream through time, different parts of the stream emerging in different periods or at different occasions. Looking ahead from where you stand, you may know too that, at every point, you will see the whole outcome stream – all that has passed and what yet will come – but that your valuation of it will be shaped by what is then passing, by the part of it you are then in. Here you may face still another kind of conflict, for you may know that your different values at different times won't all cohere.

Suppose you are deciding whether to arrange for a pension you would get many years ahead. You know that the effects would be very different in the different stages of your life. Being now young and single, you would now hardly miss the money you would be putting away. Later, when you have a family, the costs would be a burden. Finally, during retirement, the pension would yield you an income. You know that you would always keep the total outcome stream in mind, but that you would react to it differently at different points in the future – that at first you would be glad of it, and gladder yet when you retire, but that often, in between, you would be unhappy about it. This isn't a conflict like those above: you don't here want x and also y and think that you can't have both. Still, you incline toward outcome stream x and know you will later wish you weren't in it. How should you deal with this situation?

The question can be rephrased. You choose in the light of your values, but you often think of yourself as a time-extended being (extending, you hope, from now to old age). And you then pursue its values, the values of that drawn-out *you*. So the question for you is this: What should you take to be its values – *its* desires and preferences and utilities? I put this in these "take to be" terms for there isn't a fact of the matter, no values you can find or discover until you have set them up. The values of your drawn-out self are a sort of construction. They are the values you have constructed out of your values now and later, out of the values you have now and those you will have in the future.[11]

There is only a single *you*. So your extended self's desires are your current self's desires, though they cannot yet be yours where you haven't constructed them yet, for they then don't yet exist. The question you have is *how* to construct them. We spoke above of Hellman's ambivalence raising a problem of summing-up for her, a problem of establishing all-in-all values, of pulling together her different perspectives. So also on the temporal line, where we must integrate present and future. There we have to combine the values of our different time-selves, and again, the problem is *how*.

The problem is that of pulling together, of weighing and adding or somehow combining our values at different times. How should this be done? One answer is: impartially, giving all our valuations at different times equal weight. Or perhaps (to avoid double counting), fixing on just our *myopic* values at those different times – the values we think we *would* then have if we then paid the future no heed – and giving all of them equal weight.

None of us accepts this idea; very few writers have even proposed it.[12] All of us favor the here and now. We are biased against the future, and the more distant the future is, the greater our bias against it. That is, we *discount* the future. We devalue the valuations that we might make later. The weight we set on them now, from a distance, is less than the weight we expect to set on them when (and if) we make them.

This bias of ours can be justified. A bird in the hand is worth two in the bush. So that bird is worth more in the hand than it would be alone in that bush – or down the street, or next week or next month. We can be sure of the bird in the hand; all the others are chancy. And the further off they are, the chancier they are. The further off a benefit is, the less likely we are to get it, and the further off a valuation, the less likely we are to make it. Thus our bias against the future may be fully proper. It may reflect our being governed by the probabilities. And it does in fact reflect this if we discount the different futures by the improbability of our reaching them.

Still, our bias isn't always of this actuarial sort. Sometimes we are fully certain that we will live at least ten more years and yet prefer a benefit now to the same (or a larger) benefit we might have in ten years. The bias we have against the future isn't then based on the probabilities. It isn't based on what we believe are our chances of reaching it. The future needn't be distant, and our bias against it may be total. Here is a case involving a time span of only half a day. The good Dr. Jekyll knows that he will soon be the vicious Mr. Hyde. This leads him to buy a one-way ticket into the moors and to get on a train.[13] When, at midnight, he turns into Hyde, he will be where he can't do harm, and though he knows that his Hyde-self will rage, he ignores what Hyde will then want. He discounts his Hyde-self's values. Here the future (the very near future) matters not at all. Yet survival isn't in question; Jekyll *knows* he will live to be Hyde. On what basis is the future discounted in such cases as this?

We might consider the concept of a person's self understandings. Sometimes we identify only selectively with what we know of ourselves. We focus on certain actions or roles, or on certain desires or projects. We see ourselves in some and not others, identifying with *these* and not *those.* ("No, I am not a waiter. I am an unemployed actor!") On occasion, we even complain, "I am not myself today," meaning by this that what we are doing doesn't accord with our sense of ourselves.

So also, we sometimes identify selectively with our selves in the future. That is, we don't identify with all that we might become. We tell ourselves, "Yes, I may change; but if there were certain radical changes, that would not be *me* any longer." Suppose you are writing a living will. Aware that you may some day go into an irreversible coma, you ask that, should that happen, you (or that body) be allowed to die. You say, "That wouldn't be *me* in that bed. It would only be my body; there would be nothing left of *me*."

Such disavowals are puzzling, but we have to take notice of them.[14] Perhaps we should say we attend to the future, that we let it weigh with us, only where we identify with the person we expect then to be. Where we don't identify with him, we discount his values fully: we assign them no weight. To Jekyll, his future Hyde-self was alien, and so the values of that self didn't count. To the author of that living will, his possible comatose self was alien, and so its values (if any) didn't count.

There are not many cases like these, but those that we find are arresting. They all involve deep psychic changes, radical changes for the worse. Derek Parfit imagines the following nineteenth-century scene. A Russian nobleman is making plans to free his serfs (at some time in the future). He signs a postdated emancipation document and asks his wife to put her name to it too. Then he asks her to keep their commitment, even if he later changes his mind and begs her to retreat from it. He says, "I regard my ideals as essential to me. If I lose these ideals, I want you to think that *I* cease to exist. I want you to regard your husband, then, not as me, the man who asks you for this promise, but only as his later self."[15]

Jekyll could have said the same. In Jekyll's view, Hyde wasn't Jekyll; he was just a "later self," a man in whom Jekyll "ceased to exist." About to turn into Hyde for good, he wrote, "This is my true hour of death, and what is to follow concerns another than myself."[16] Jekyll might have also said that Hyde was a different *person*. He might have said, in Parfit's words, "He is one of my later selves, and I am one of his earlier selves. There is no underlying person who we both are."[17] Still, again, these matters are dark, and we oughtn't to make too much of them. Perhaps some future self of ours won't be the person we are today, but it will be the same individual, the same man or woman, the same human being. Otherwise we couldn't report that later self as *our* later self. We couldn't speak of seeing *ourself* as a different person then.[18]

Sometimes our bias against the future reflects the probabilities of our staying alive. Sometimes it may reflect our self-understandings instead. There may, however, be something else too. We discount the future often just because it still is ahead, displaying a naked bias against it, a naked bias toward *now.* We postpone the dentist. We can visit him next month. Perhaps we will die before the time comes and so avoid the drill altogether, but that is not why we stay away. Rather, we indulge a pure *time-preference* here: better later than sooner, as far as discomfort and pain is concerned, even where nothing else speaks for that. We discount our future aversion to pain and discomfort because it is future.

Likewise with future attractions to pleasure. Often we discount them also just because they still are ahead. Here is a much-discussed case. Homer's Odysseus, sailing home, knew that he soon would be passing the Sirens and that these ladies sang a song of such an enticing beauty that all who heard it were overcome and drawn to the shore and disaster. He knew he too would be seized with desire and would want to head for shore. So he arranged to prevent that: he had himself tied to the mast. He restrained his future self, disallowing what it would want, though he would have let himself go were he already hearing the song. He acknowledged that self as his own; lust wasn't foreign to him. (He didn't say, "That won't be me!") Still, he fully discounted its values.

Odysseus's sort of discounting is common. Think of the smoker trying to quit who flushes his cigarettes down the drain. Think of people on a heavy diet who put night locks on their refrigerator doors. They know that the Sirens will call them, that the craving is only hours away, but wanting now not to yield to it then, they arrange to thwart it. Or what is going on may be this: these people know they soon will be deaf to all but the call of the moment, and their flushings and night locks don't express a current time-preference but the hope of defeating one later, when they hear the call. Either way, what they are doing involves a pure time-preference discounting.

Can a pure time preference be justified somehow, or does it reflect a bias that, as Ramsey says, "is ethically indefensible and arises merely from weakness of the imagination"?[19] Ramsey's opinion is shared by many, but there are others who disagree.

Here is one way to consider the question. I have a pure time-preference for *x* where my now wanting it counts more with me now, in the present, than my wanting it later (even where I am sure I will want it). I have what might be called a pure *self*-preference where my wanting it counts with me more than does *your* wanting it. Self-preferences are common, and we think them defensible, at least in many situations. I think it defensible to give more weight to *my* wanting *x* than to *your* wanting *x*. Why then should it be *in*defensible to give more weight to wanting it *now* than to wanting it *later*? If I may have a pure bias toward *me*, why not a pure bias toward *now*? (It may be said that *I* am not *you*. True, but so also, *now* isn't *later*. Why should my later self's being *me* be "ethically" more compelling that my present self's being *now*?)[20]

Again, are pure time preferences "ethically indefensible?" This is a question of ethics, of ethics broadly conceived. It asks about how we *ought* to shape up, what kinds of preferences would be *proper* for us, what values a person *might* or *should* have. We can here leave this question open. (We will return to it in Chapter 7, where we will leave it open too.)[21]

A final elaboration. My report of some of these cases may have been too brisk. I assumed that, in them all, the agents expected some changes in their values. But perhaps the Russian nobleman thought that his values would stay as they were, that he thought he never would cease to want to free his serfs. Say that he also thought he would always want to avoid financial ruin. It may be that he was guarding against a change in his *understandings:* he saw what he was planning to do in terms of freeing his serfs but knew he might come to see it instead in terms of ruin and so back off.[22] Likewise perhaps for the pensioner; he may have thought that his values were firm but that his understandings would change. He may have expected himself at seventy to focus on the outcome stream's benefits, not its costs, and thus expected his then-understandings to activate values now dormant for him.

Let a case be of such a sort, the agent expecting his future understandings to activate values he now puts aside. How can (or how should) his present understandings adjust to that expectation? How might people establish a unity of understandings for their cross-time selves? Our discussion of value discounting carries over here, people here discounting the importance they later will set on their understandings. Sometimes (as perhaps in the pensioner's case) they discount importance weights by the unlikelihood of their getting to set them – by the improbability of their living long enough to have the understandings involved. In other situations (like the nobleman's story), the discounting of an understanding reflects a disavowal. ("*That* understanding doesn't count. It would not be *mine!*") And perhaps sometimes pure time preferences enter in this context too.

4 BACKWARD REACTIONS

The local team wins the championship. Neither one of us benefits or will pay for the team's having won. Still, you cheer and I grumble. The difference derives from this, that you wanted the team to win and I wanted it to lose. What you wanted to happen did, and so you are pleased: you are gratified. What I wanted to happen didn't, and so I am not: I am disappointed. Gratification and disappointment are backward-referring reactions. They presuppose our having wanted this or that to happen.

We can take the point further. The more you wanted x to happen, the more you are gratified when it does. Also, the more you wanted it to happen, the more disappointed you are when it doesn't. The more you wanted good weather tomorrow, the more you are pleased when the sun comes out, and the more you are disappointed when it rains. (Better: your disappointment over *x*'s not happening reflects how much more you wanted *x* than what happened instead, and so too for being pleased, except that there you are contrasting *x* with what *might* have happened.)

How you now *see* what happens also enters. Say that you wanted a million dollars. You will not be gratified if it is sent you by the company that insured your child's life. You won't because you won't see that money as you saw what you wanted before. You wanted the money qua wealth (or perhaps simply qua money). You will now see it qua a payoff for the death of your child, and you never wanted it qua such a payoff. Gratification is being pleased because we got what we wanted, but only if we see what we got as we saw what we wanted.

Being gratified and being disappointed also reflect the prior probabilities. You wanted it to be sunny, and you are gratified when it is; this we just have noted. You are even more gratified if you thought good weather unlikely. And if you wanted good weather and thought it likely but then it rains, that is extra-disappointing.[23] Indeed, if you believed all along it would be sunny – if you assigned this the probability 1, you won't be gratified at all when it is. (You will enjoy the weather, but its having turned out good won't itself then please you.) Likewise, you can't be disappointed by what you expected beforehand.

These matters need some attention, or we may be misled. Granted, our rational choices are based on how we now value the outcomes, and our present values often take account of our values later. But our then being gratified will not put us into a circle. Those later values will be independent of whether we are gratified then. (We may perhaps then value *x* highly though we won't have been gratified by it, having fully expected it.) The moral is that our concept of values isn't that of being gratified or pleased, that our logic of rationality isn't a born-again hedonism.[24]

There is also a second sort of backward-referring reactions. In this, we focus not on having wanted what now happened (or didn't) but on what we did in the past that led to the present situation. Often too we look ahead and try to anticipate these hindsight reflections. In particular, we often reflect on what we may later wish we had done – on what we then may wish we did *now* (as we then will see it). We think of the regrets we may then have, and we try to avoid them. Hellman reports that she told herself, "Make sure you come out unashamed." But shame had been on her mind from the start; looking ahead to being ashamed of having taken a cautious line had got her to turn against caution.

Sometimes the prospect of facing regrets affects the choices we make. At other times, our mind is made up but looking ahead still gives us pause. Though we decided that, all in all, x is the best we can do, we foresee that we may regret it, and so we have second (and third, and fourth) thoughts. Hamlet's case is a warning, as Hamlet himself was aware: "Thus conscience does make cowards of us all; and thus the native hue of resolution is sicklied o'er with the pale cast of thought." Still, nothing obliges us to keep rethinking. We can leave a closed issue closed; we can (unlike Hamlet) be *resolute.* When is it only conscientious to dwell on regrets we may come to have (when is it due to "conscience"), and when is it neurotic? When should we stop to reconsider and when should we be resolute? There is no general answer.

Suppose we haven't yet chosen, and that we know that we would regret our choosing this or that option. Should that now stop us from choosing it? Some writers hold that it should, that our future selves have a veto. They speak of *ratification,* a choice of some option being *ratified* – being allowed to go forward – only if we don't expect to wish we chose differently when we looked back. They propose that we choose only options that we are able to ratify. Where rationality leaves us no ratifiable options, they counsel against being rational.[25]

Choose only what you could ratify – choose for who you expect to be! This assumes you expect to have just a single future self, or that you think your selves in the future (tomorrow, the next day, the day after, etc.) will all agree in what they regret. Or that every future self with regrets must be given a veto. None of this sounds right. Suppose that we retreated a bit, committing ourselves to looking only to our next-future selves: choose for who you expect to be next![26] This perhaps would be doable. But if you are Jekyll and soon will be Hyde, should you really look to Hyde to endorse the choices you make? Should you now, as Odysseus, still calm, defer to your sex-crazed, next-later self?

Deferring to the future is one extreme here. The other extreme is ignoring it. Never mind your future – choose for who you now are! Do what you can by your present values and take up your regrets when you have them. This can't be the right approach either, not for a person who is rational, for such a person considers the outcomes, and his regrets will be part of the outcomes: they will be caused by what he now did. A rational person considers the outcomes, his regrets along with the rest, and the values he now sets on them determine how he now chooses and acts. He isn't moved directly by any regrets he foresees, but he may be moved by how he now values the prospect of having them.[27] How *ought* he to value such prospects? How should he now value his looking back later with these or those regrets? There is no general answer here either.

Likewise where the agent attends to his later being glad of what he did, though here there is no danger of brooding, of endless rethinking, of the loss of "resolution."[28] Suppose he foresaw his applauding himself for taking option x. Should the applause make a difference to him? Should a rational person's choices reflect his foreseeing of hindsight-gladness? We can answer as we just did, that they needn't reflect it directly, that they only need to reflect how he now feels about later being glad. His then being glad is a part of an outcome he foresees, and so an outcome-attentive chooser is bound to take it into account. *How* should he take it into account? What weight ought he to give it? These questions too must stay open.

5 CONTINGENT SELVES

We may later be glad we did what we don't now want to do. A special problem sometimes is found in cases of this sort. Suppose you incline against option *x* (or don't now care either way) but that you know your taking it would change you – that it would make you glad you took it. You would then be glad that you took it, but only because of the change in your values you induced by your taking it. Ought your later being glad nonetheless now count in its favor?

This has been called the *boot-strapping* problem, and also the problem of *endogenous changes.* We saw that it troubled Bettelheim when he first thought of analysis. Bettelheim knew that analysis would change him and that the change would be such as to make him glad he went into it. How should he have responded to that? Should the prospect of endorsement by values he knew would be boot-strapped have counted for him? I incline to ask "Why not?", though there is something worrisome here. Boot-strapping looks like a way of letting your actions establish their own validation. We return here to an issue that we met in Chapter 1. Does attending to boot-strapped values accord with maintaining integrity?

Integrity says, "Come out unashamed." Make sure you do what squares with your values. Yes, but what if what you are doing determines how you will value it later? Suppose you at first inclined against *x* but that you knew that your taking that option would lead you to later approve what you did. Suppose you valued your foreseen approval so much that you ceased to oppose taking *x*. Would integrity let you proceed? Again we might ask, "Why not?" If the prospect of your approval canceled your initial opposition, your values now accord with your *x*'ing and the values you foresee will accord with it too. So you can't come out ashamed.

But take a more difficult case. Suppose that Bettelheim had to choose between entering analysis and entering the Church. Suppose he liked neither option he had (that he disliked them equally) but that he knew that, either way, he would, in time, adapt to his life and be glad of his choice. And suppose that, knowing this, he still liked neither option. What would integrity have let him do there? Neither option squared with both the values he had and those he foresaw. Perhaps he ought to have attended to his summary, cross-time values, to the values of his cross-time self. Still, how might he have done that?

How should you choose for your cross-time self where what that self will be (its values) will depend on the choice you now make? There may be no uniquely good answer. Here are two approaches, neither clearly better than the other. You might consider which of your options has a prospect that your cross-time self in it would rank no lower than the prospects of any others – and then choose one of these options. Or you might consider which of your options has a prospect that your cross-time self in it would rank no lower than your cross-time self in any other would rank that other prospect – and make your choice from those options.[29]

The first approach is to choose a course such that, were you on that course, you (your extended self) would not wish you were on any other. The second is to choose a course on which you would be no less happy than your other contingent selves would be on any other. Let *x* and *y* be the only options you have. On the first, the *no-grousing* idea, you could choose *x* only if your then-consequent self ranked the prospect (the outcome) of *x* no lower than it ranked that of *y*. On the second, the *happiness* idea, you could choose *x* only if your *x*-consequent self ranked the prospect of *x* no lower than your *y*-consequent self ranked the prospect of *y*. (The two approaches come to the same in the usual sort of case, in which the values of your consequent self are unaffected by how you choose now.)

A fresh scenario will help. Suppose you are having trouble finding a job in your line of work; pending a suitable offer, you are driving a cab in New York. An offer comes – from the Black Hills of Wyoming. You are sure there won't be any others, so it is either Wyoming or the taxi. You were born and bred in the city. Country living now puts you off, but you know that, were you to move, you would soon get to like it, and would indeed enjoy your life better than you would had you stayed in New York. Still, if you stay in New York, you will prefer the life you will have to the one you rejected. What ought you to do in this case?[30]

On the no-grousing idea, you can stay in New York, for you wouldn't then wish that you were living in Wyoming. On the happiness idea, you should move to Wyoming, for your contingent Wyoming self ranks your (contingent) life in Wyoming higher than your contingent New York self ranks your (contingent) life as a cabbie. I incline to the second idea, barring any disavowals of the future involved ("That wouldn't be *me* in Wyoming"). Why not reach for happiness (again, if you see it as *yours*)? Why not do what would make you happiest if you did it? But notice that the happiness idea points you to Wyoming even if you would, if you moved, continue to prefer a life as a cabbie – even if you would then wish you were back in New York. Being happy doesn't rule out grousing![31]

6 SELF-KNOWLEDGE

Our discussion of people's conflicts has made use of two metaphors. In speaking of Hellman, we talked of perpectives. We spoke of Hellman's perspective from prudence and her perspective from principle. In speaking of Jekyll, we talked of two selves, of Jekyll's public, well-behaved self and his vicious

Hyde-self. We spoke of Bettelheim's different selves, before and after analysis, and of your arranging a pension, your next-year's self, your self the year after, etc.

The metaphors were different, but the ideas were not. We could have put it all either way. Instead of speaking of Hellman's perspectives, we might have spoken of different part-selves – of Hellman's prudent and principled selves. Or we might have not spoken of selves but of perspectives only, of Bettelheim's from before and from after and of yours from today, from next year, and from the years after that. Either way, the point was this, that we live with value conflicts, sets of desires or preferences that we think incompatible. Also, these conflicts we have being *inner,* that the opposing value stances are all somehow ours.

Or *are* they all ours? – that is one question. What makes a stance (a part self) ours? Were the values that Hyde had Jekyll's, or was Jekyll right to reject them? Was he right to disown them, to say they were those of "another than myself"? In the case of the pension, are our values at age forty already ours at twenty? Or should we say that they aren't ours yet, that it now is up to us whether we *make* them ours? A person who lives for the present only is often said to ignore his own interests. Is that indeed what he is doing, or are the values that he pursues the only ones that are his?

A deeper (prior) question is this: What counts as someone's part self? Or in the other terms we are using: What is a perspective? A part self doesn't have mental states. It has no beliefs and values of its own. It is a value stance of the agent's, a kind of juncture of values, of values that cohere at any point in time. A part self speaks with one voice only, at least at any point in time – it is, in that sense, *univocal.* Still, does each univocal ranking single out a part self? What about a ranking from a perspective the agent rejects?

Another (yet deeper) question: What exactly is a *whole* self – "whole" in the sense of marking a *person*? A whole self can't be just a collection of distinct part selves. Some whole selves may not have parts; and besides, not every collection of part selves composes a whole. *Your* part selves and *my* part selves together form a collection, but they form no single, whole self. They are not *one person*'s parts.

A narrower way of putting this: What is *our* whole self? What do we shape when we shape up? And who are the *we* that do the shaping? What is the *me* in *my* part selves? We assume there is always some agent, some over-all managerial unit, at least in the usual situations.[32] Was there not a single Hellman, a single person taking different perspectives? Yes, but what does that say about her? What makes a person whole and distinct?[33]

I will pass these issues by. Nothing I have been saying constrains the way we must think about them. But here is yet another question; on this, what preceded does force our hand.

Can we always know our own self – our whole, managerial self? Is self-knowledge always possible? This now has to look unclear, for, again, what *is* our self? But take the question to be asking what we can know *about* ourselves. Can we know what we have chosen and what we are going to choose? And can we know what we now want and what we believe and our present understandings: Can we know our own reasons? Most people would say that we can. Still, some self-knowledge can't be had. Some knowledge is out of reach.

The proof is short and simple. Suppose we now have a certain option. If we knew we would choose that option, we would think we would take it. This because its being an option means that we think we are free to take it, that we would take it if we wanted it (as we understood it) – and having chosen it, we *would* then want it (as we then understood it). But our now thinking that we will take it would rule out its being an option. What we think we are going to do isn't an option for us; it isn't a *live* option we have. So we can't be said to choose it, for we can only choose from our options.[34] If some *x* is an option for us, we can't know beforehand that we will choose it. We can't even *believe* we will choose it. (Start the proof with "If we believed . . ." in place of "If we knew. . . .") Likewise if *x* is not now an option but will be at some future time: we can't now know or believe we will choose it.[35]

We can know how others will choose, and others can know how we will. But we can't know how *we* will be choosing (not even if we are told by the others!). We can't foreknow our own choices, not because they will be capricious or because we lack the right data but because our concepts exclude it, our concepts of options and choices. We can't because we cannot choose where we face no issue, and because we face no issue where there is no uncertainty for us – and there *would* be no uncertainty if we knew our choice beforehand. We can't foreknow our own choices, because they then wouldn't be choices.

I have held that reasons are causes, that (at least in typical cases) our reasons establish what they are reasons for. A corollary is this, that if we knew we had a reason for *x*'ing, we could (in most cases) expect to *x*. Add that to what we just have argued and this follows too, that (in most cases) we can't know our reasons for our still-ahead choices. Or rather, that we can't know those reasons if we know our reasons to be causes.[36] Suppose we did know our reason for some future choice. We could then expect to make it; we could *believe* we would make it. But again, we *can't* believe that: we can't have forebelief of our choices. So we can't know our present reason for any future choice. If in fact we have such a reason, we can't fully know ourselves here and now.

Notice how much this leaves us. We can't know our reasons for the choices we will make, but we can *have* reasons for them. And we can know those reasons *later.* We can then know the reasons we *had* for the choices we *made*. Also, the above refers just to choices: we can't foreknow our choices or the reasons we have for them. To the extent that what we do depends on how we chose, our foreknowledge of our actions thus has limits too – as does our knowledge of our reasons for our actions. But we can act without having chosen. So we can often foreknow our actions. And we can know our reasons for those future (non-chosen) actions.

We cannot know what we will choose. And if we say that reasons are causes, we can't know our reasons for the choices we will make. Still, we can often foreknow our actions and our reasons for them. And we can know what reasons we had for our choices after we make them, when we may want to explain them. So though we can't have total self-knowledge, we aren't much the worse off for that.

5

OTHER PEOPLE

IN what preceded, we chose alone. Or rather, our choices were independent of how any other people chose. We didn't look over others' shoulders to see how they would be choosing, or if we did, we thought that these others weren't then also looking over ours. Sometimes our choices are *not* independent of those of others, and that can raise problems.

1 CONFRONTATIONS

In Jean-Paul Sartre's play *No Exit,* a man and two women are locked in a room. The man, Garcin, is a brute and a coward and wants the approval of the older woman, Inez. She, however, despises him, and indeed men in general, and hungers for Estelle, who wants only Garcin. This is how it will have to be for these three for all time, for it turns out that they are in hell and this is the punishment set for them. Garcin's (and Sartre's) conclusion is that "Hell is other people!"[1]

Their predicament is bad enough, but why that sweeping conclusion? Why are other people hell and not just certain engagements with them? For Sartre, hell is dependence on others. What Inez wants she cannot get unless Estelle does her part of it, and what Estelle wants she can't have either if Garcin holds back. Likewise for what Garcin here wants; only Inez's approval will do. In every room of Sartre's hell, each person wants something he cannot get except from certain others, who refuse. People sometimes avoid frustration; sometimes, in real life, the others consent. But people are always dependent on others and so they are always vulnerable.

Let us drop the idea of hell. Let us also turn the story into a messier kind of involvement. The people in *No Exit* know exactly what they want. Their minds are fully made up, and so their dismal situation raises no choice problems for them. Let us make it more of a challenge by changing it so that they each must choose.

Here is our new *No Exit.* Each of the three still has to move toward (reach for) one of the others, but each now must choose toward which other to move. (Say that Garcin, like the two women, is out for sex only – too late for approval!) Each still has a favored outcome, but each also has a next-best in mind. Each of them knows that what will happen isn't up to him or her alone, that none of them alone can bring about what he or she wants. (Garcin knows that he alone can't bring it about that he and Inez get together.) And each of them thinks that both of the others are choosing. We can here speak of *co-agency.* We might also speak of these people as being involved in a *confrontation.*

Again, each agent has to choose while thinking that the others must too, and each knows that what will follow will be jointly caused. To simplify, say that each of them knows at least some of the options of the others and what outcomes would be yielded by this or that combination of actions. Also, that no one sees any point in trying to get to agree, to compromise ("On Mondays, we'll pair up *this* way, on Tuesdays we'll do it *that* way, . . ."): none of them thinks any agreement would be kept. Also, finally, that no one thinks that his or her action is any clue to the others', that if he or she were now to do *this,* this or that other would (probably) do *that.*

The problem each faces is which way to go, given that the others are asking the same – or given that he now *thinks* this. Suppose that in fact they aren't. Perhaps they don't even know he is there, or they already have chosen, or they think *he* has chosen. Say that Garcin is just as above but that Inez is blind to his presence or that her mind is made up. They are then not in a confrontation, though Garcin thinks that they are. Still, what he thinks has to count for him; he must act on what he believes. So the logic of confrontation has to apply here too.

Our *No Exit* story is fiction, but such problems are common in love and also where love has no place. Lawyers on opposite sides of a case, preparing their briefs, are fully co-agents. They not only think they are in one but are in fact in a confrontation. So too are opposing politicians preparing their campaigns. So too are the managers of business firms competing for sales in a market and the players in certain games, like poker or checkers or chess. Such games provide a good metaphor, and the logic of confrontation is therefore called the theory of *games.* We will soon turn to that special logic, but let us first draw some distinctions.

2 DIFFERENT KINDS

To begin with, the number of agents. Some confrontations involve just two people, some (as in *No Exit*) three, some a much larger number. The logic we want must allow for any number. Still, the two-person case is the simplest, so we will here keep mostly to that.

Next, some cases are *zero-sum,* and others are not zero-sum. In the former, the sum of the benefits to all those involved is zero, however these people act.[2] Or we can sometimes put it like this, that whatever is gained by the gainers is lost by the others involved. In a *two*-person zero-sum case, the more one person wins, the more the other loses. We might put it most usefully this way, that these people have opposite preferences over every pair of outcomes.[3] In *non*-zero-sum situations, the benefits and losses don't always cancel. The agents might there all do better in some outcome than in some other, or some do better and the rest no worse.

In a zero-sum situation, every benefit is at someone's expense. Where there are more than two people involved, some of them may form a coalition. But since the sum of the benefits must be zero, what the coalition gains for its members has to be paid for by those left out. Sometimes joint effort may make a pie larger, and everyone might then benefit; but where the size of the pie is fixed, no one does better unless others do worse. In a zero-sum confrontation, people can only arrange some way of dividing the fixed stock of benefits.[4]

A two-person zero-sum case is based on a total opposition of interests – we might again speak of conflicts, here of *outer* conflicts. The far extreme of *non*-zero-sumness rests on a total harmony or consensus, all the parties ranking all the outcomes alike. Romeo and Juliet agreed all the way. They should have had an easy time of it, but where the agents must act alone, neither knowing what the other is doing, even such cases sometimes end badly. (Things did end badly for Romeo and Juliet, and just for this reason, because they acted alone.) The challenging cases are those that combine some conflict with some consensus, conflict regarding some pairs of outcomes, consensus regarding the others.

We will say that the outcome of a set of actions is *jointly superior* to another such outcome if all the parties prefer it to that other,[5] or if some prefer it and the rest are indifferent. We will say that the second outcome is then jointly *inferior* to the first. This suggests a distinction between *rationally hurtful* and rationally *non*hurtful confrontations. In confrontations that are rationally hurtful, the outcome of everyone's acting rationally might turn out to be jointly inferior to some other that was possible for them. That is, if all act rationally, each person might do worse than he could have if they weren't all rational, or some may do worse while no one does better. A *non*hurtful confrontation is one in which the outcome of everyone's acting rationally can't be jointly inferior to any other.

To focus our thinking on all this, consider first the familiar scenario known as the Prisoners' Dilemma. In that, two prisoners are told that there is no evidence against them, that they will be sentenced solely on the basis of whether they confess. If they both do, they will both get a heavy sentence. If only one confesses (saying that both of them did it), that person will be released, the other then getting a *very* heavy sentence. If neither confesses, they will be held just overnight. Neither of them cares what happens to the other. Each cares only about keeping out of jail; the shorter the sentence, the better. Each must now choose whether to talk or be silent, each in the knowledge that the other must too.

Let the prisoners be Adam and Eve. Their options appear in Figure 1, Adam's two options as the rows, Eve's two options as the columns – *S* is staying silent, *T* is talking. The numbers refer

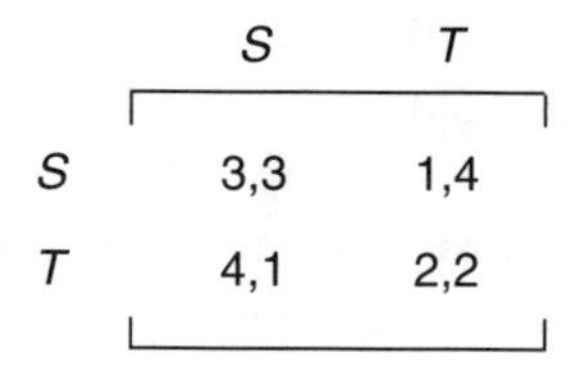

Figure 1

to the outcomes of joint-takings of these options, the first number in each pair being Adam's ranking of that outcome, the second being Eve's (the larger the number, the higher the ranking). Let *S,S* be both of the agents staying silent, *S,T* be Adam's staying silent while Eve talks, etc. The outcome of a joint action will be reported in angle brackets. Thus $\langle T,S \rangle$ is the outcome of Adam's talking while Eve stays silent, etc. Notice that both Adam and Eve prefer $\langle S,S \rangle$ to $\langle T,T \rangle$; their preferences not being fully opposed, their confrontation isn't zero-sum.

An option is said to be *dominant* for a person if he prefers the outcome of taking it to the outcome of taking any other, however his co-agents act, or prefers it in some contexts of their acting and is indifferent in the others. Both Adam and Eve have dominant options; for each of them, T is dominant. (Each would do better by talking than by staying silent, whatever the other did.) A person who is rational in our Chapter 3 sense will take a dominant option where he has one[6] – such options are always maximizing. The Chapter 3 concept is basic, so if both Adam and Eve are rational, both of them will talk. But the outcome would then be $\langle T,T \rangle$, which is jointly inferior to $\langle S,S \rangle$, so their confrontation is rationally hurtful. If they both act rationally, they will both wish they both hadn't.

The Prisoners' Dilemma is a two-person interaction. The corresponding many-person case has been called the Tragedy of the Commons. Say that many farmers are sharing a commons for the grazing of their cattle. The commons can barely sustain the number of cows that now are on it, and each additional cow sent to graze diminishes its yield. But the benefit to each farmer of sending out an additional cow outweighs his share of the cost of the damage that particular cow would cause, this whatever the other farmers do – however few or many of them send out a new cow of their own. Each farmer thus has a dominant option: send out another cow. If all are rational, they all will do that, and the commons will be destroyed, an outcome jointly inferior to the outcome of their all *not* doing it. So this too is a hurtful confrontation.[7]

A third scenario is the game of Chicken. In the original two-person version, two cars are speeding toward each other down the middle of a highway. Each driver can either swerve (S) or continue (T). Each expects the best outcome (a win) if he continues while the other swerves, and the worst (a collision) if they both continue. Each expects the next-to-worst outcome (shame) if he swerves while the other continues. The Chicken involvement appears in Figure 2. Here $\langle T,T \rangle$ is jointly inferior to every other outcome, but neither agent has a dominant option.[8] Is this involvement rationally hurtful? Would the hurt in $\langle T,T \rangle$ result from the agents' being rational? That depends on

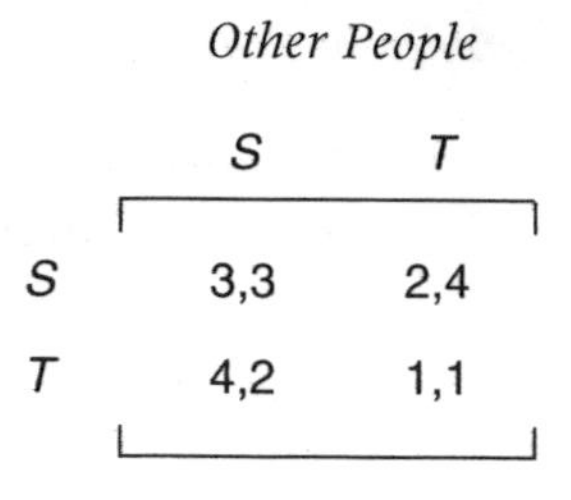

	S	T
S	3,3	2,4
T	4,2	1,1

Figure 2

what it is rational for these people to do. Common sense shouts "Swerve!", but would a sound logic endorse that?

Finally, the *No Exit* story, as revised above. Since there are three people here, the outcome matrix is three-dimensional. Still, only four distinct outcomes are possible – *a:* Garcin and Inez getting together (with Estelle left out), *b:* Inez and Estelle getting together (Garcin left out), *c:* Estelle and Garcin getting together (Inez left out), and *d:* none of them joining with anyone else (each moving for one who moves for another). Say that Garcin most wants Inez, but better Estelle than no one. Estelle most wants Garcin, but better Inez than no one. Inez most wants Estelle, but a man would disgust her, so better alone than with Garcin. Garcin's ranking of the four outcomes is this: *a,c,b/d* (*a* is best, *c* is next-best, *b* and *d* tied as worst), Estelle's is *c,b,a/d,* and Inez's is *b,c/d,a.*[9] Outcome *d* is jointly inferior both to *b* and to *c.* But only Inez has a dominant option (reaching for Estelle). How should the other two choose? What would be rational for them?

3 GAMES

We made some simple suppositions when we first spoke of co-agency. Suppose now further that each of the agents knows all the options of each of the others and what outcome would be yielded by what combination of actions. Suppose each knows all the others' rankings of the possible outcomes.[10] And suppose that each is rational in the one-agent (Chapter 3) sense – that each will maximize where he can – and that each knows this is true of the others. Also, that each knows that the others know this, and that each knows that the others know that the others know, etc. – this last is called the *common knowledge* assumption.[11] Their confrontation is then called a *game*. (Our examples of confrontations all were examples of games.)

How do rational people choose in a game situation?[12] First, suppose each has a dominant option. No problem here: each is one-agent rational, so each will choose his dominant option. There needn't be any problem either where no option is dominant for some agent. Say that, in a two-person game, x is dominant for Eve but no option is dominant for Adam. Since Adam knows Eve's preference ranking and knows that she is (one-agent) rational, he knows that she will take x. He will therefore choose some (one-agent) rational response to her x'ing. Or say that Eve has no dominant option but, all considered, x is best for her. If Adam knows this, he expects her to take it; and so again, no problem.

Suppose that none of this holds. If Adam assigned some probability to every combination of actions by the others and set utilities on all the outcomes, he could maximize expected utility. One or more options would come out best, and he would take one of these. But this too may be blocked. Adam may know that the others involved are trying to outguess him (and each other). That may leave him in the dark, not only unable to predict the others' actions but unable to assign precise probabilities to their various combinations.

In Chapter 3, we spoke of choices under vagueness, of choosing where we assign no precise probabilities (or utilities) but only probability (or utility) ranges. We considered the concept of *rationalizable* options, an option being of that sort if some constriction of all the ranges to points would yield it an expected utility at least as great as the one yielded (by the same constriction) to any other. The suggestion was that a rational person facing vagueness would choose such an option. Where the probabilities range the whole distance from 0 to 1 and no option is dominated by any other (none is dominant over even one other), every option is rationalizable. This implies that, in many games, a rational person might choose any option.

Must we stop with that? Consider the game in Figure 3. Adam again is choosing rows, Eve is choosing columns, and

	S	*T*	*U*
S	3,7	9,1	1,9
T	5,5	7,3	6,4
U	4,6	2,8	8,2

Figure 3

both of them have three options. The game here is zero-sum, Eve's preferences being the opposite of Adam's. Let the situation be one of total probability vagueness. Each of Adam's options is then rationalizable for him, and each of Eve's is for her. Still, notice that the worst-possible outcome for Adam if he takes *S* is ⟨*S,U*⟩, that the worst outcome if he takes *T* is ⟨*T,S*⟩, and that the worst if he takes *U* is ⟨*U,T*⟩. Of these three, the best is ⟨*T,S*⟩. Thus *T* has the highest security level: *T* is Adam's maximin course. ⟨*T,S*⟩ is the best of the worsts for Eve too, so *S* is *her* maximin course. Though each of their options is rationalizable, *T* stands out for Adam and *S* stands out for Eve.

The game in Figure 3 is a two-person, zero-sum game. Say that some outcome in such a game is (as here) the best of the worst for both agents. Where they are moving toward that outcome, neither person alone will change course. Were he to shift while the other stayed on, he would not benefit by it. A pair of actions of which this is true (one action of Adam's, the other of Eve's) is called an *equilibrium* pair.[13] Or we might say that a pair of actions is *in* equilibrium if each is a best response to the other – if each yields its agent an outcome he can't improve on given what the other person is doing. Where two people's taking certain options would be in equilibrium, we can speak of the options themselves as an equilibrium pair. Extending this to the many-person case, a set of actions (one for each agent) is an equilibrium *set* where, if anyone departed from his while all the others kept to theirs, that person wouldn't benefit by it.

One more technical term: let us call a game *blank* for an agent where he is totally uncertain (vague) about what the others will do, where he assigns only the full probability ranges to their possible actions – except insofar as what they will do follows from the structure of the game itself and these others' being one-agent rational.[14] (A Prisoners' Dilemma is blank for both parties; each is certain of what the other will do, but only because each knows that *T* is dominant for the other and that this other is rational.) The central principle of the logic of games is that, if a game is blank for a person and has some single equilibrium set, rationality directs him to take the option that is his part in that.

In a two-person, zero-sum game, this just comes down to maximining. In other sorts of games, it doesn't, or at least not always. In the Prisoners' Dilemma (Figure 1), the maximin option for both agents is *T* and the equilibrium pair is *T,T*. Though this is not a zero-sum game, each agent's equilibrium option is still also his maximin option. But consider Chicken (Figure 2). The maximin option of each agent is *S*, but *S,S* is not an equilibrium pair; if either driver swerves, the other does better to continue straight ahead. And in our revised *No Exit*, both his reaching for Inez (*I*) and his reaching for Estelle (*E*) are maximin options for Garcin, both *G* (reaching for Garcin) and *I* are maximin for Estelle, and *E* is maximin for Inez, but neither *I,G,E* (as in Sartre's hell) nor *E,I,E* is an equilibrium set. In the former situation, Garcin would do better to turn to Estelle, who is reaching for him; in the latter, Estelle would do better to turn to Garcin, who is reaching for her.

A rational person equilibrates (in a game that is blank for

him): he chooses an option in an equilibrium set. But both in Chicken and in *No Exit* there are *two* equilibria – in Chicken, they are *S,T* and *T,S;* in *No Exit, E,G,E* and *I,I,E*. In such cases, would either do?

Where there are several equilibria, some are sometimes excluded by simple dominance – plus perhaps the common knowledge of that. One or more of the agents may have a dominant option that excludes certain equilibria.[15] Or one of them may have a dominant option, and the others (or some of them), knowing this and deleting the options it dominates, may find that they have dominant options of their own given what then remains.[16] One or more rounds of such deletions may exclude certain equilibria too. For instance, both Garcin and Estelle know that reaching for Estelle is dominant for Inez; counting on her to do that, each of them sees that he or she can't do better than to reach for the other. This leads them to *E,G,E* – the *I,I,E* equilibrium is excluded. (The outcome is then the best possible for Estelle and the next-best for the others: Hell has been outsmarted!)

Still, what of cases in which no equilibrium is excluded this way. Look at the game in Figure 4. This has two equilibrium pairs, *T,S* and *U,U,* neither of them excluded by dominance but

	S	*T*	*U*
S	5,8	8,9	1,3
T	7,7	4,4	2,2
U	6,5	9,1	3,6

Figure 4

one of them jointly superior to the other, this in the sense that both Adam and Eve prefer ⟨*T,S*⟩ to ⟨*U,U*⟩. Here it sounds right to say that Adam should choose *T* and Eve should choose *S*. This suggests that we keep to equilibria that are neither excluded by dominance nor jointly inferior to any that isn't excluded – call such a nonexcluded and nonbested equilibrium an *admissible* equilibrium. Where there is only one equilibrium (as in Figures 1 and 3) or only one not excluded by dominance (as in *No Exit*), this reduces to choosing the option that is the agent's part in that.

In a game with two or more equilibria, one of them admissible and the others not (as in Figure 4), this idea directs the agent to his option in that admissible equilibrium. Where several equilibria are admissible (as in Chicken), it lets him take his option in any one of these. Sometimes, in this last sort of games, if different agents move for different equilibria, they may establish an outcome that is jointly inferior to some (or to all) of those aimed at. Games in which this might occur are, in our sense, rationally hurtful (and thus Chicken *is* hurtful). But a game with several equilibria can be hurtful even if only one is admissible; in Figure 4, only *T,S* qualifies, but *S,T* (which is *not* an equilibrium) is jointly superior to that.[17]

This logic holds just for cases in which a game is blank for the agent, and not every game is blank for every person involved. A person for whom a game isn't blank has to go by the logic of risk. Look again at the game in Figure 4 and suppose that Adam thinks that Eve thinks he will take *S*. Thinking this about her, he thinks that the game isn't blank for her and that, being one-agent rational, she will take her *T*. Whether or not he is right about her, the game is now not blank for *him*. Being one-agent rational too, he will ignore the equilibria here and will maximize: he will take *U*.

It may also be worth noting that not every game has equilibrium options. Consider the game in Figure 5. This has no equilibria. Whatever the outcome will be in this case, either Adam or Eve will regret what he or she did to bring it about. If the outcome is ⟨*S,S*⟩, Adam will wish he had taken *T*. If it is ⟨*T,S*⟩, Eve will wish she had taken *T*, etc. The equilibrium logic has nothing to tell us about games without equilibria. Though per-

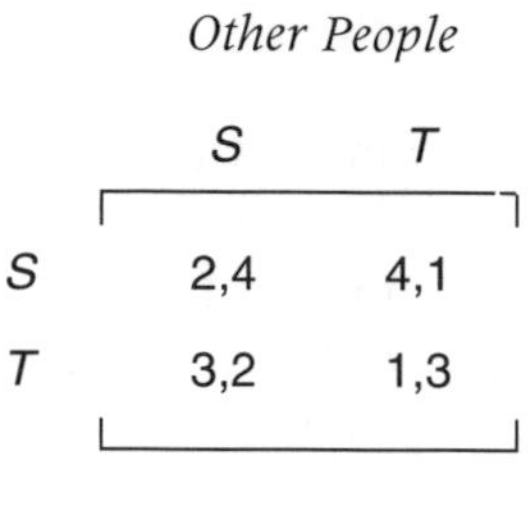

Figure 5

haps we can let it be saying that, in such games, any choice would do (any choice of an option that isn't excluded by dominance considerations).[18]

4 COOPERATION

In a zero-sum situation, no outcome is jointly superior to any other. Thus none is jointly inferior, which means that a game that is zero-sum can't be rationally hurtful. Rationality can make for trouble only where interests aren't fully opposed. In this last kind of situation, everyone may wind up sorry, and often that is foreseeable.

We have met several sorts of cases. In the Prisoners' Dilemma, the equilibrium logic directs each agent to *T*, but $\langle T,T \rangle$ is jointly inferior to $\langle S,S \rangle$ and both agents know it. In the commons story, if each of the farmers is rational, each will send out another cow, and that, as each knows, will ruin them all. Look also at Figure 4. Here rational Adam will go for *T* and rational Eve for *S*, and so they will forfeit $\langle S,T \rangle$, which they both prefer to $\langle T,S \rangle$. Individually rational agents can make a collective mess of things. And they often can't avoid it even where they all foresee it.

We might put this in different words, in terms of cooperation. People cooperate where, all together, they act in a way that benefits all (relative to some outcome they might have had instead), or where the juncture of their actions benefits some without hurting any – where they go as far as they can in that direction.[19] To pin this down, consider an outcome that is jointly superior to some other and isn't jointly inferior to any.

Such an outcome might be called a *cooperative* outcome. An option that allows for such an outcome is then a cooperative *option,* and we can say that people are *cooperating* where they take options that, all together, will yield such an outcome. In Figure 4, ⟨*S*,*T*⟩ is a cooperative outcome, and Adam's *S* and Eve's *T* are thus cooperative options. And since these are the only such options, only if Adam took *S* and Eve *T* would they be cooperating. We have seen that rational people often (as here) won't cooperate. They will often *not* cooperate even where they know they all will be sorry (and wish they had all cooperated).

The reader may say that it serves them right, that this comes of their being selfish, of their thinking of themselves only. Each of the farmers around the commons pursues his own interest in the issue before him, and our Adam and Eve do too, but the point here cannot be that doing that doesn't pay. Pursuing one's interests isn't even always selfish. Whether people are being selfish depends on how they see the outcomes and on how they value them – *what* their interest in them is – as they currently see them. They are selfish where they see them in terms of the distribution of benefits in them and are indifferent regarding the possible distributions to the others. And besides, *un*selfish people, people who are altruistic, needn't cooperate either.

For instance, look at the game in Figure 6. Rational Adam here will take *S* and rational Eve will too, for *S* is dominant for

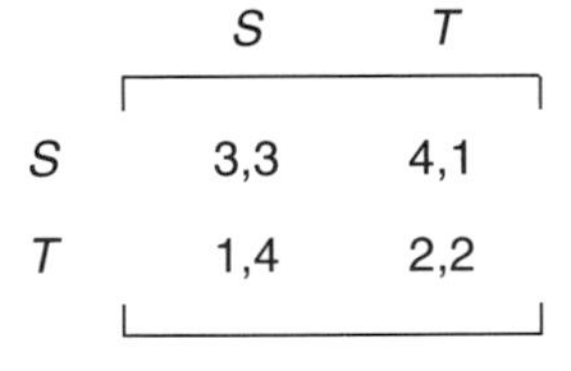

	S	*T*
S	3,3	4,1
T	1,4	2,2

Figure 6

each. And they will be cooperating: they won't both be sorry later – *neither* will be sorry. From their values (in the matrix) alone, we can't tell whether they would be selfish.

Let them each now come to see the outcomes in a new light. Let each come to see the outcomes in terms of how the other would fare in them, and let each suppose that this appears in the other's valuations. Or let each look at Figure 6 and note how they *both* would fare. Adam then sees the outcome ⟨*S*,*T*⟩ as *I will do as well as I could but Eve will do very badly.* He sees ⟨*T*,*S*⟩ as *I will do badly but Eve will do well,* etc. Eve sees the outcomes correspondingly, in a way that takes in Adam. If each of them cares about the other, each will switch to a different ranking, one that reflects (in part or in whole) how the outcomes matter to the other. This means that their game will change; it may even get to be that of Figure 7. Here they would both be unselfish enough – they could not be more so. Still, if they are rational,

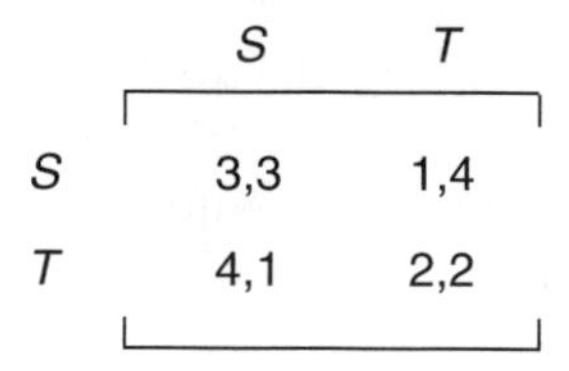

	S	*T*
S	3,3	1,4
T	4,1	2,2

Figure 7

they would each take *T*, for *T* would be dominant for each. And thus they would forfeit ⟨*S*,*S*⟩, which they both would prefer to ⟨*T*,*T*⟩. They would not cooperate, their being unselfish – their being *altruistic* – having led them into a Prisoners' Dilemma.[20] (Figure 7 is the same as Figure 1.) Selfishness can make for trouble, but so (as here) can *un*selfishness. This shows us that selfishness isn't the problem; the problem is rationality.

Perhaps the problem has to do only with rationality as we have defined it. Could we somehow redefine it so as to get in the clear? Consider adopting this idea, that, if a game is blank for an agent, rationality directs him to a cooperative option, if he has such an option in the game – that it calls for an equilibrium only where he has several such options or none. This would have Adam taking *S* in the Prisoners' Dilemma. But *T* is dominant for him there, and our basic one-agent logic therefore directs him to *T.* Unless we fiddled with that logic too, we would offer conflicting directives. Since our one-agent logic alone sometimes blocks cooperation, we can't avoid the problem just by revising the logic of games.

So we seem to be stuck with this, that rationality sometimes excludes cooperation. Some games are rationally hurtful, and the way to avoid the hurt is to avoid those games or to change them. Again, let the game be a Prisoners' Dilemma (Figures 1 and 7). Adam might try to improve his prospects by offering to reward Eve if she took *S* or by threatening to punish her if she took *T.* If she believed his threat or promise, the game they are in would change; it might become that of Figure 8. The outcome of

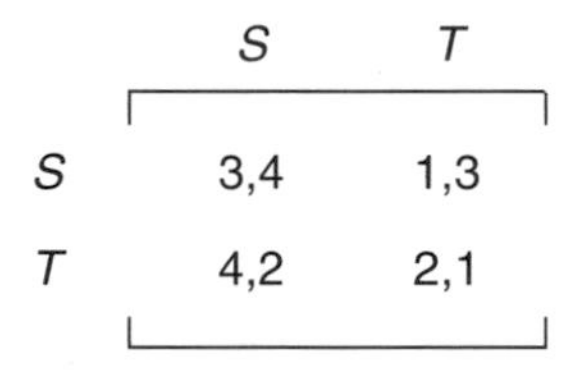

	S	*T*
S	3,4	1,3
T	4,2	2,1

Figure 8

this, if both are rational, would be ⟨*T,S*⟩, a cooperative outcome and the best possible for Adam, though not very nice for Eve. But Eve may also threaten Adam or promise him some reward, and this, if each believed the other, might give them the game of

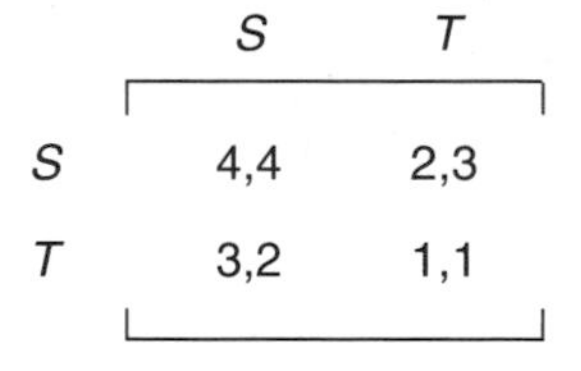

	S	*T*
S	4,4	2,3
T	3,2	1,1

Figure 9

Figure 9. In this too, if they are rational, they would cooperate – they each would take *S.*

They would have arranged for taking what were their cooperative options in the Prisoners' Dilemma, this by changing the game so that it isn't a Prisoners' Dilemma any longer. The new game matrix (in Figure 9) would reflect their new expectations. But why should they have these expectations? Why should either believe the threats or promises of the other? Threats and promises are costly to keep, and by the time that either knows how the other acted, the game will be over.[21] Convinced that the other won't go to expense just to keep his or her promise or threat, each is likely to disbelieve the other. But then they are back in the Prisoners' Dilemma, where they know they both will be sorry.

This may overstate the case. We may think that, in the long run, a policy of keeping one's word makes good sense and that it therefore is at least possible that the other has such a policy. That may argue against rejecting the other's threats and promises and so perhaps support a policy of cautious cooperation. Here we encounter a sort of games that deserves a section of its own.

5 SUPERGAMES

One way out of a hurtful game is to change the game's outcomes. In a Prisoners' Dilemma, this may come to changing them so that $\langle T,S \rangle$ is no longer best for Adam and/or $\langle S,T \rangle$ no longer best for Eve; the agents try to do just that by making threats and promises. A second way is to change the issues, to get the agents to change their options.

The writings of Michael Taylor explore this second possibility.[22] Taylor studies a variety of games, but he keeps mainly to Prisoners' Dilemma, taking that to be the pattern of many rationally hurtful games. Suppose that the parties in a two-person Dilemma know that they will meet again, that the present encounter is only the first of many just like it. Suppose that neither knows how many such meetings there will be. They may then be brought to stop asking whether now to take *S* or *T* and to ask instead what policy they should follow in the whole sequence of meetings. Where that has become the issue before them, they are not facing a series of games, of separate Prisoners' Dilemmas, but a single, complex game – the Prisoners' Dilemmas *super*game. That is, they are facing a game whose options are long-range strategies for a series of what *would* be Prisoners' Dilemmas if they then still had to choose.

But won't they *have* to choose? Suppose that, somewhere in the course of the sequence, one of them saw the current situation as a simple Prisoners' Dilemma, *not* as a round of a supergame. He committed himself at the outset to some long-range strategy, but he now has lost that commitment. This means he now must face the issue of what to do in the Dilemma he is in. Should he take *S* or *T*? In such a case, he has to choose.

Yes, but a person needn't lose his initial determination. He can keep a closed issue closed; he can be what we called *resolute*.[23] He can see each situation as a round of a supergame in progress, as he did when he planned ahead, when he chose his strategy, and he can also continue to want to follow that chosen strategy. A person who is thus resolute, whose mind is made up and resists being changed, faces no issue at any point in the sequence. The choice of a strategy, a *super*choice, ties such a person's hands. It excludes all further choosing (as long as his mind-set persists).[24]

Back now to prisoners Adam and Eve, this time facing a supergame. Let Adam expect to know in each round what Eve did in those that preceded. This lets him choose to govern his action in every round by what Eve did before. Not only can Adam now choose to take his cooperative move in every round he will reach or to *defect*, to *not* take it, every time – Taylor labels these options C^∞ and D^∞ (in our notation, they are S^∞ and T^∞). He also can choose to tit-for-tat: to start in round 1 with *S*, and then, in every subsequent round, to do as Eve just did. Taylor calls this option *B*.[25] Or Adam might be more cautious, starting in round 1 with *T*, and then, in every later round, doing what

Eve had just done; this Taylor labels B'. Many such strategy options are possible. A person's supergame strategies (or most of them) make what he does in each round depend on what the other did in those that preceded.

Which of his strategy options will a rational Adam choose? That depends on how he ranks the outcomes of all the junctures of his options and Eve's, the outcomes of all their strategy pairs. The outcome of any such strategy pair is a sequence of pairs of actions, or rather, it is the sequence of the *outcomes* of those action-pairs; it can be written $\langle\cdot,\cdot\rangle, \langle\cdot,\cdot\rangle, \langle\cdot,\cdot\rangle, \ldots$. The outcome of Adam's taking B and Eve's also taking B (of both tit-for-tatting) is thus $\langle S,S\rangle, \langle S,S\rangle, \langle S,S\rangle, \ldots$. The outcome of Adam's taking B and Eve's taking B' is $\langle S,T\rangle, \langle T,S\rangle, \langle S,T\rangle, \ldots$. The outcome of B',B' is $\langle T,T\rangle, \langle T,T\rangle, \langle T,T\rangle, \ldots$.

How will Adam rank these outcomes? That depends on the values he sets (*presently* sets) on how he would fare in the future, in each of the rounds to come. The more the future now matters to him, the larger his *discount factor*, the lower will he now rank all outcomes offering him benefits today or tomorrow he would be paying for later.[26] A discount factor is assumed to be the same from each round to the next: where d is Adam's discount factor, he values some benefit x rounds in the future at d^x times its worth to him now. It ranges from 0 to 1, the two extremes here not included – the future might matter hardly at all, or middling somehow, or almost as much as the present. If the future matters enough, Adam will prefer $\langle S,S\rangle, \langle S,S\rangle, \langle S,S\rangle, \ldots$ to $\langle T,S\rangle, \langle T,T\rangle, \langle T,T\rangle, \ldots$, the prospect of the long run of $\langle T,T\rangle$'s offsetting the appeal of the initial $\langle T,S\rangle$. Thus if the future matters enough, he will rank the outcome of B,B above the outcome of D^∞,B.

Still, which option will Adam choose? A supergame is a game, and so the game logic applies: if the game is blank for him, he will choose an option in an admissible equilibrium. Taylor notes that various equilibria are possible in a supergame of the Prisoners' Dilemma: D^∞,D^∞ is always an equilibrium, and several other junctures of strategies are equilibria where the agents' discount factors satisfy certain conditions. The details needn't concern us; Taylor's basic conclusion is that where the discount factors of both agents are sufficiently large, *B,B* and D^{∞},D^{∞} are equilibria and all the other strategy pairs he thinks would be considered are not.[27] Since only *B,B* is admissible (it is jointly superior to D^{∞},D^{∞}), each of the agents will therefore choose *B*. It follows that, where their discount factors are sufficiently large, both agents will cooperate in every round.

The agents here undo their Dilemma by changing the issues that brought it on. They reject their initial options and make their choices in a supergame. But what warrants their leaving their game, their turning away from their current issues and taking up supergame options? What warrants that change in perspective?

Suppose that two people know they are facing a long run of identical Prisoners' Dilemmas. Say that they are brought to see that they *might* make a supergame of it. They then face a setting-up game, a game in which each agent decides what he will do in what follows, whether he will choose anew in each separate encounter or will superchoose (all at once) for the series. Each thus has two setting-up options – call them *I* and *J*. On Taylor's theory, both *I,I* and *J,J* are equilibria (where the discount factors are sufficiently large) but only *J,J* is admissible.[28] Rational people in a setting-up game will therefore choose *J;* they will set up the supergame. If the theory is correct, rationality not only directs both agents to take *B* in a Prisoners' Dilemma supergame. It dissolves their initial Dilemma by imposing the supergame on them (where they see that as a possibility).

The question remains, is the theory correct? Say that a supergame has been set up for a Prisoners' Dilemma. Is it true that *B,B* is the only admissible equilibrium in it? Whether or not it is depends on what, besides *B*, the agents might choose – on the *other* options they have. Taylor discusses some alternatives to *B* (he comments on *B′*, C^{∞}, D^{∞}, and some others), and he holds that the options he studies "include those which are most likely to be considered . . . by real players."[29] It seems to me he is wrong on this point, and that the options he overlooks undermine his conclusion.

Imagine a willful exploiter, Adam, who insists on enjoying some number, say m, of unpenalized defections. Another way put: Adam insists on m one-sided (free) cooperations from the other. His strategy, W^m, is to defect at the start until he has defected m times while the other cooperated, and then to shift to B. Let there be some other person, Eve, whose patience leaves her vulnerable, who will cooperate m times at the start, whatever Adam is doing. (Perhaps she will hope to bring him over.) Her strategy, V^m, is to cooperate in each of the first m rounds – to turn the other cheek $m-1$ times – and then to shift to B. (Since Adam will have just defected, this will turn that cheek once more.)

It can be shown that W^m,V^m is an equilibrium pair if the two agents' discount factors are sufficiently large. Indeed, there may be many such equilibria, since for every finite m there are two numbers (between 0 and 1) such that, if Adam's discount factor isn't less than the first and Eve's isn't less than the second, the W–V pair for that m is an equilibrium. All of these are admissible even where B,B is an equilibrium too,[30] for Adam prefers the outcome of any W^m,V^m to the outcome of B,B and also to the outcome of any W–V pair with a smaller m, and Eve has the contrary preferences.[31]

Being willful and being vulnerable are familiar dispositions, and so we have to let W^m and V^m be options that typical "real players" might have. But letting them be options undoes the uniqueness of the B,B pair – it keeps that from being the sole admissible equilibrium. Which means that the long-run logic gives us less than we hoped for from it. Where the future matters enough, it is rational to choose B in a supergame and so to be ready to cooperate all the way. But this doesn't let us say that no other strategy ever is rational.[32]

6 GETTING REAL

It doesn't always pay to be nice. Thinking that Eve has B as an option, Adam might choose B himself. But if she thinks he has V^m as an option, Eve (being rational) may well choose W^m. The outcome would then be $\langle S,T \rangle$, $\langle T,T \rangle$, $\langle T,T \rangle$, $\langle T,T \rangle$, ... Nice guys often finish last, though sometimes the *not*-nice ones don't do much better.

We hoped to find something else, that rational people who look to the long run will be drawn to cooperate with each other. Still, perhaps we failed to find this only because of too narrow a focus. We have been keeping to supergames that are what we called *blank* for each agent. These are cases in which each agent is fully uncertain of what the others will do.[33] Where a supergame of the Prisoners' Dilemma is blank for one of the people involved and that person supposes the other to have V^m as an option, rationality doesn't restrict him to tit-for-tatting, to Taylor's B – this we just saw. But the assumption of blankness is often totally unrealistic. Which way does rationality direct us when we don't make that assumption?

Here we can apply the results of Robert Axelrod's famous computer shoot-out.[34] Axelrod invited game theorists to submit computer programs for a Prisoners' Dilemma supergame tournament. The tournament would be run as a round-robin. That is, each program would be matched against every other (and against itself), a match to consist of 200 meetings of the Prisoners' Dilemma sort. Each meeting would be scored – S,S would yield 3 points to both of the programs involved, S,T would yield 0 to the S-taking program and 5 to the T-taking program, etc. The sum of a program's points in a match would be its score for that match, and the program with the highest average score over all matches would be the winner.

Tit For Tat won the tournament. Axelrod announced the results and offered an account of why some programs did better than others. He then invited submissions for a second, similar such tournament. Many of the programs in that were prepared in the light of lessons drawn from round one. Thus, says Axelrod, "The second round presumably began at a much higher level of sophistication than the first round, and its results could be expected to be that much more valuable."[35] Tit For Tat won again.

The lessons of the first round were confirmed in the second. One lesson was that it pays to be *nice* – that is, never the first to defect, never the first to take *T*. Another was that it pays to be *forgiving*, to have some propensity to take *S* after the other took *T*. The second tournament suggested also that it pays not to be *too* forgiving, that it pays to be *retaliatory*, which Axelrod defines as "immediately defect[ing] after an 'uncalled for' defection from the other."[36] Combining all this: it pays to be nice and to reciprocate both *S*'s and *T*'s. In brief, it pays to tit-for-tat.

The matches simulate supergames between people, and so this general, summary lesson should extend to the real-life games like them. In these games, the discount factors are large (in the tournaments, they all were 1) and the agents have the same set of options and each believes that the other party is equally likely to choose any one of them. The bit about the agents' beliefs brings out that these games aren't blank for these people. The equilibrium logic designed for blank games therefore doesn't apply. What applies is the logic of risk, which calls for people's maximizing, for their doing what they think will pay best. And the message of the tournaments is that, very often, tit-for-tatting pays best.

Clearly, it doesn't always. Whether it does in this or that case depends on the options in the mix, though Axelrod notes that tit-for-tatting works very well in a variety of contexts. Often too, our real-life games aren't like those in the tournaments. Sometimes the discount factors are small, the future "casting too small a shadow" and rationality thus calling for T^{∞} (for *T* all the way). And sometimes we don't think it equally likely that the other will take this line or that. Rationality may point us to tit-for-tatting even where we don't, as where we think it very likely that Eve will tit-for-tat. Not so where we think it is likely that the other will randomize: where we think he will toss a coin each time to decide between *S* and *T*, rationality points us to T^{∞}.

In real life, of course, we seldom think the other party will randomize. And we often expect the other will tit-for-tat, or we think that likely. We may think that the other thinks that we have read somewhere that tit-for-tatting is rational and so will now do it and that he therefore will too. Or that he thinks we will tit-for-tat because we were brought up to do this and so will do the same, or that he here will tit-for-tat because of *his* upbringing. Or (most often) we think he will do that because of his conduct in previous games, either with us or with others. Why we think it doesn't matter; what matters is that we think it. For often that then argues for our tit-for-tatting too.

What is left of Sartre's dictum that "hell is other people"? Sartre was thinking of interdependence and of frustration all around. Yes, we often frustrate each other. But often also we tit-for-tat, which, where the others are doing the same, locks us into cooperation. Sometimes such lock-ins can't be arranged. Where we don't think beyond the present or are facing a total blank, the story still can end badly. Nonetheless, "hell" is too strong. Other people can be a nuisance, a headache, and even a curse, but we can learn to live with them. We can even make friends with them and deal with them then as with friends. We will turn to some topics now that let us reflect on that.

6

SOCIAL CHOICE

PEOPLE don't always choose alone. Sometimes a person makes his choices where certain others are choosing too. And sometimes a person chooses *for* others. The choices that person then makes are grounded in the interests of others. Here we enter new territory.

1 PROXIES

We have seen that rational people sometimes can't cooperate. They sometimes can't cooperate even where they know they will be sorry if they don't. Perhaps they even agreed to cooperate. The problem they then have is how to get their agreement to stick.

More precisely, the problem they face is how to prevent reneging. Each of the prisoners in the (one-meeting) Dilemma will agree to stay silent, but each intends to renege, and each expects the other to do it if he can get away with it. So also in various other games. We spoke of these matters above, and we spoke of threats and promises and of long-run strategies. There remains a possibility we have not considered. The parties who have reached an agreement might ask someone else to carry it out. They might appoint an executor to act for them all jointly – to do for each person, in his or her stead, what that person had agreed to do. Call such a person a *proxy.* Where the people involved have a proxy, none of them can renege. Their agreements will be kept, whether they like it or not. And, of course, these people know this: they know their agreements are binding.[1]

Setting up a proxy is costly. It calls for a prior agreement to share the setting-up costs. There isn't yet any proxy in place, so why should people keep *that* agreement? Why should they pay their agreed-upon share if they would do better *not* paying whether or not the others pay theirs? (Here is another Prisoners' Dilemma!) Let us sidestep this issue. The proxy is installed; never mind who paid. Whatever agreements these people will reach, the proxy is going to implement. We can now ask this: To what will rational people agree where they can count on implementation?

They might agree to cooperate. That would clearly be in their interest where they have a proxy if, acting alone, without an agreement, they would all wind up sorry. For instance, with a proxy around, the prisoners in the Dilemma might agree to cooperate. They might, that is, agree to stay silent, to take their options *S* in Figure 1. Their proxy (their lawyer) would then take over. He would announce they have nothing to say, and they would soon be free. The farmers around the commons might agree to cooperate too, to keep to the cows that they have. Their proxy (the village cowherd) would then let in just the cows they agreed on, and the commons would survive.

Sometimes there are no cooperative outcomes and so there can't be cooperation, but let us speak only of cases in which cooperation is possible. Rational people won't always agree to cooperate in such cases, not even where they have a proxy who would make their agreement hold. This because some of them wouldn't be sorry if there were no cooperation. They would do better if there weren't. Look at the game in Figure 10. Here $\langle S,T \rangle$ and $\langle U,U \rangle$ are the only cooperative outcomes, but Eve (column chooser) can be sure of something better if she takes her option *S*. She prefers each possible outcome of her taking *S* to either cooperative outcome. Why then should she agree to cooperate by taking *T* or *U*?

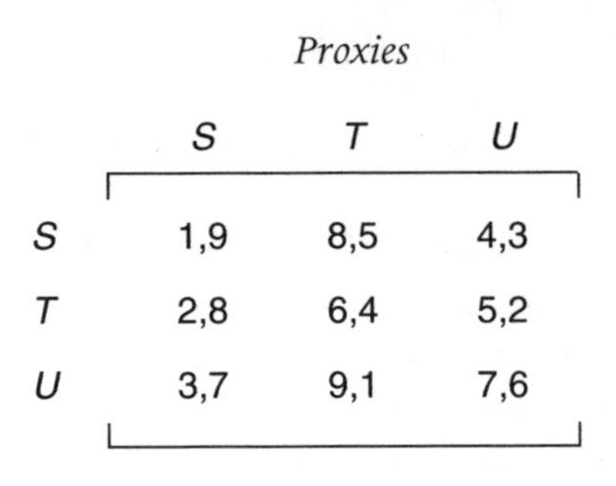

	S	T	U
S	1,9	8,5	4,3
T	2,8	6,4	5,2
U	3,7	9,1	7,6

Figure 10

Look also at Figure 11. This is a three-dimensional matrix, Adam choosing rows, Eve choosing columns, Lilith choosing levels, the upper level (left) being Lilith's *S* and the lower level her *T*. (The first of the numbers refers to Adam's ranking, the

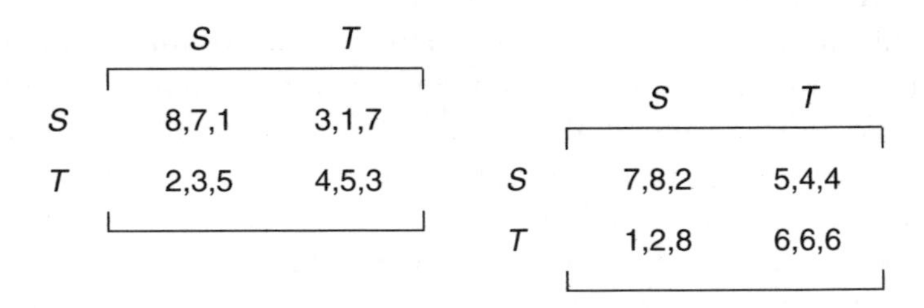

	S	T
S	8,7,1	3,1,7
T	2,3,5	4,5,3

	S	T
S	7,8,2	5,4,4
T	1,2,8	6,6,6

Figure 11

second to Eve's, the third to Lilith's.) Here ⟨*T,T,T*⟩ is the sole cooperative outcome, but Adam and Eve would both do better if they both took *S*. For in that case, whatever Lilith did, the outcome would be the best for one and second-best for the other, while ⟨*T,T,T*⟩ is only third-best (for each). Why should Adam and Eve agree to cooperate here with Lilith?

This sort of situation is sometimes described in terms of the concepts of *blocking* and the *core*. A possible outcome of a game is *blocked* where some person or the members of some coalition – of some partnership under a (binding) agreement – can assure themselves of something better than they would get in that outcome, where they can be sure of doing better whatever the others do. In the game of Figure 10, both $\langle S,T \rangle$ and $\langle U,U \rangle$ are blocked by Eve. In that of Figure 11, $\langle T,T,T \rangle$ is blocked by the coalition, the partnership of Adam and Eve. Again, in the game of Figure 10, Eve can act in a way that assures her of doing better than in $\langle S,T \rangle$ or $\langle U,U \rangle$ however Adam acts. And in the game of Figure 11, Adam and Eve, acting jointly (or being *acted for* by the proxy), can both be sure of doing better than in $\langle T,T,T \rangle$. The outcomes that aren't blocked by any agent or coalition of agents are said to be in the game's *core*, and rational people who have a proxy will agree only to bring about an outcome in the core. That is, a rational person will agree to some arrangement only if he couldn't assure himself of doing better, either alone or in some coalition.[2]

Thus even where an agreement would be binding, rational people needn't agree to cooperate. They *won't* agree in any game whose core contains no cooperative outcome. Perhaps they also won't agree in games whose cores contain several such.[3] They *might* agree to cooperate where the core contains one such only. A Prisoners' Dilemma allows for only one cooperative outcome, and that outcome is in the core (and the only item in it). In the farmers' commons case too, there is only one cooperative outcome and it is in the core. If a proxy is standing by, the people in these games might agree to cooperate. But in Figure 10, only $\langle U,S \rangle$ is in the core, and in Figure 11 only $\langle S,S,T \rangle$, and neither of these is a cooperative outcome. Agreements may be reached in these games, but not any agreements to cooperate.

Sometimes rational people can't get to cooperate with each other. Sometimes they won't even *agree* to cooperate, not even where a proxy would act for them all. Still, suppose that they have a proxy. Perhaps he won't wait to be told what to do but will assume some initiative. (Perhaps the others will want him to do this!) If he judges that some outcome would in some sense be collectively best, he will then impose that outcome even if the others have reached no agreement. Here we encounter a whole new topic, for the proxy's taking over sets up a new sort of chooser. Or better, it sets up a chooser for whom we need a new logic of choosing.

2 SOCIALITY

We will describe the proxy agent as a *social* proxy, and we will speak of the issues he faces as his *social* issues. The options composing a social issue will be his social *options*. We might take such an option to be a juncture of people's possible actions – for instance, Adam's doing *this* while Eve does *that* while Lilith does *that* . . . , or perhaps the proxy's acting *this* way for Adam and *that* way for Eve and *that* way for Lilith . . . . But it is more usual to let the proxy's options be the *outcomes* of such junctures, situations that no person alone (aside from the proxy) could arrange. Thus a full report of a proxy's option for a whole society would identify "the amount of each type of commodity in the hands of each individual, the amount of labor to be supplied by each individual, the amount of each productive resource invested in each type of productive activity, and the amounts of various types of collective activity, such as municipal services, diplomacy and its continuation by other means, and the erection of statues to famous men."[4] In our more narrow contexts, one social option would be this: Smith having sent out an extra cow, the other farmers all holding back. Another would be Garcin and Estelle's having gotten together (leaving Inez out). Better, in terms of the proxy's doings, the proxy's options are to *bring about* this outcome, to *bring about* that one, etc.

Again, the proxy might be thought of in either of two ways, either as coordinating what people do – that is, as doing it *for* them – or as bringing about the outcome of some juncture of what they might do, and it is more usual to think in the latter way here. The proxy has to choose and act in the light of these people's values. How ought he to go about that? Suppose that the people are the citizens of some country and that the proxy agent is their national government. Say that the project is to set up some public health-care program for them. The different programs being considered are the social options. Which of them should be established? How should the agent (or agency) choose, given the citizens' values?

We need a few more new special terms. The grounds that a person has for his choices are certain beliefs and desires he has. Still, what he thinks are the values of others sometimes enter indirectly insofar as these values figure in what he believes and wants. Stretching our use of "grounding" a bit, we can speak of a proxy's choices as other-person or *socially* grounded. The choices he grounds (again, indirectly) on how some others value his options will be called *social* choices, and their social grounding will be their *sociality* – this for a start, we will firm it up shortly. How should the values of other people constrain the proxy's choices? This is the question of the logic of sociality, a topic largely unexplored except in connection with politics. In that limited context, however, we have what is known as *social choice theory*.[5]

Here is the sort of thinking involved. Let the proxy face an issue composed of a number of social options, and let there be n people for whom that agent is choosing – these people are his *constituents*. Suppose that each of the n constituents ranks the options in some order of preference. The problem of instructing (of constraining) the proxy, of keeping him properly responsive to the others, is the problem of finding some rule that, for every n-fold set of rankings of the options at issue, specifies some set of these options as the proxy's *choice set* – as the broadest set of them from which the proxy may choose.

Strictly, many such rules could be offered. The problem is to fix on just one, to find a rule that we can endorse, one that expresses the way we think a person *should* be attentive to others. The usual course is to present a number of formal conditions or principles, conditions that (the presenter holds) must be met by any proper rule. The project then is to find some rule that satisfies them all. This is not a promising project, for the principles most often proposed turn out to be incompatible. No choice rule accords with all of them – this surprising result was the initial theorem of social choice theory.[6] One response is to stick to our principles and to despair of sociality. A better response is to reverse the project, to find some rule we are willing to endorse and to adapt our principles to it.

Here is one possible rule: let the proxy's choice set be the set of those of his options that are not jointly inferior to any others. This allows for the proxy's choosing to impose a cooperative option where there is one. That is, this rule always yields a choice set containing all the possible cooperative options, though it may also contain certain others (those that are neither jointly inferior nor jointly superior to any others). Where people's preferences are such that nothing would count as cooperation for them, the choice set contains every option at issue, and, in such cases, any choice goes.

This rule is certainly weak. The options in a choice set it yields may be very dissimilar, and we may not want to leave the proxy free to pick any one. Some critics will also take the occasion to fault our concept of cooperation. They will say that cooperative options, as we have defined them, often offer too little, that they can be improved on, and that we therefore shouldn't always let a proxy choose from among them.

We have defined cooperation in terms of jointly superior options and so in terms of preferences only. Suppose we spoke instead of utilities and of *collective* superiority. There could well be *non*cooperative options in which the people involved would do better, collectively speaking, than in any cooperation. Though some might do worse than if all cooperated, others would do better – possibly many others. That is, a *non*cooperative option might have a greater utility-sum than any cooperative option. This suggests a refinement. We could let the choice set be determined by an n-tuple not of preference rankings but of utility assignments. And our choice rule could be this, a kind of utilitarianism: let the proxy's choice set be the set of those of his options whose utility-sums are not exceeded by the utility-sum of any other option. The proxy here must choose some option that maximizes the sum of his constituents' utilities.

There are those who reject this rule too. They fault it for taking no account of what the constituents might have done for themselves. We spoke above of the concept of the core. Those who think in terms of that concept hold that people should never be made to settle for less than they could have got on their own or in some coalition with others.[7] This idea calls for a different sort of refinement, for the core is a choice set determined not by an n-tuple of utility assignments but by an n-tuple of preference rankings plus what was possible prior to the entry of the proxy, this last bringing out what these people alone and their various coalitions could have provided for themselves.

Think again of the problem of establishing a public health-care program. And suppose someone is wealthy enough to assure himself privately of good medical care, of better care than he would have got on any public cooperative plan (in our sense here of "cooperative"). Or say that some private group insurance would be better for those in some group than any (in our sense) cooperative option, and that these people make their own arrangements, ignoring the others involved. These others might lack the means to set up a system for themselves and so might be left uninsured. The advocates of the rule of the core are willing to deplore this situation, to call the self-insurers ungenerous, even heartless. But they insist that no proxy (no government) may require generosity, that no person may be made to diminish his welfare just to augment some others'.[8]

Still other rules have been proposed, some of them having the proxy attend to more complex or more selective functions of people's values, sometimes to functions of their *conditional* values – of what they *would* want if . . . . Jean-Jacques Rousseau argued for following what he called the General Will (a unanimity of certain conditional values), and, more recently, Patrick Devlin argued for following the Public Morality (a different sort of unanimity).[9] All these ideas are narrowly focused. They refer only to social choosing on the political scene, and they threaten to get us entangled in political ethics. So enough about games and proxies. Let us move back a step or two and take in the larger picture.

3 SOCIAL GROUNDING

A social agent need not be a proxy. His issues needn't be social issues – that is, his options needn't be social, needn't be outcomes of junctures of actions taken for other people. What is essential is only this, that his choices be grounded in what he thinks are the values that others set on his options.[10] There needn't even be more than one other. In a just-one-other case, a social agent's choices reflect what he thinks are that other's values. In a many-others case (two or more others), how he chooses reflects his combining of what he thinks these others' values – or we might say, his *summation* of them, perhaps some *weighted* summation. There is very little consensus on how one ought to sum others' values, on what counts as a summary valuation: call that a *social* valuation.[11] But put that ought-question aside. We don't need an answer to it to say whether someone is choosing socially, whether how he is choosing is grounded in how he has summed others' values.

In Chapter 4, we introduced some closely related ideas. Our lives extend through time, and we foresee our values changing. So we have to sum over time in order to choose for our cross-time selves, one sum for each of our options – often a weighted (discounted) sum. We also must sum over different perspectives for our all-in-all selves (again, one sum for each option). A rational person looks to the outcomes of what he might now do. If he has summed the values he sets on these foreseen outcomes, the summary values are then his own and he chooses in their light – in the light of the *cross-perspective* or cross-*time* values he sets. A social person chooses in the light of his *social* valuation, a summing-up of the values set by certain others on his options (*his* summing-up, thus *his* social valuation), one such sum for each option.[12] What is different here is this, that he needn't first adopt that as his own set of values (though he might).

We can now fix up the concept of sociality with which we began. Let us put it this way, that a person who is social wants to take an option ranking highest in his social valuation and that he chooses an option he thinks is of that sort. He chooses an option he thinks of that sort and then acts it out. This takes us beyond our basic idea of his going by the values of others only insofar as it has us speaking of these others collectively.[13]

A person's social choices are thus *grounded* in a particular way. They are made in the context of a certain sort of belief-and-desire, a belief-and-desire reflecting the values of other people (collectively). The belief and desire are the agent's own, but they refer to the values of others, to what these others want.

Recall that rational choices too are defined by the agent's grounds, though of course the grounds there are different. Neither our concept of sociality nor that of rationality has to do with peoples' reasons, with what in fact is moving them. A social agent may be moved by a desire for money or fame; his reasons then focus on these. What still makes him a *social* agent is that he has others' values in mind, even if only marginally, that (besides wanting the money or fame) he wants to do what matters most to these others and thinks he is doing that. Say he wants also to bring about an outcome that is best in his own estimation and thinks he is doing that too. He is then also being rational, having both social and rational grounds for what he is doing. Being social allows for being rational in the same issue, on the same occasion.[14]

A social agent attends to others, to how the others value his options. But the others may value his options differently under different descriptions. To which of the values they set on his options does a social agent attend? To those that they set on them under descriptions expressing these or those understandings – yes, but *whose* understandings? He might attend to how the others value his options as he understands them or as they themselves do. These two ways of attending to others provide for two sorts of sociality. Let us call them *simple* and *compound* sociality.

Some examples may help. In the movie *A Sunday in the Country,* a successful painter, an old man now, is visited by his daughter. His paintings are calm and sunny, but she finds a startling canvas, full of passion, in the attic. He tells her he painted that long ago, when he was trying out new approaches. He saw his work then as experimentation, but his wife saw it differently and (he knew) was secretly grieved that, at thirty, he still was unsettled – still, as she saw it, was floundering. Reacting to this, he put fervor aside and adopted his present style.

What the painter did was grounded in his concern for his wife. He wanted to give her what she wanted, and he believed that a style of painting that was more stable, more established, would do that. So the way he then chose to paint expressed his sociality. But did she want him to stop his experiments? She never thought of art in those terms. If her husband considered only which of his options, *as he saw them,* she favored, her distress might not have struck him. He wouldn't have found himself drawn to change and might have remained the painter he was. But his attachment to her went deeper. He wanted to take the option she favored as *she* saw his options and so he settled. His story reveals not *simple* sociality but *compound* (or *deep*) sociality.

Here is a many-others case. Say that you hold some political office and have to design a general policy for the allocation of dialysis machines (artificial kidneys). You can't give a machine to everyone who needs one – there aren't enough for all. You propose a system providing for the people most likely to benefit, and you do this on the grounds that your constituents want such a program.

There is this complication: the people most likely to benefit are those whose work isn't physically stressful, and this means that your policy favors the middle class and the rich. Your constituents know this, and though they approve of policies that will do the most medical good (and grant that your policy will), this is not how they see the policy you are proposing – they see that as unfair. If you here pursue that policy on the grounds that these people are for it as *you* understand it (in terms of the medical benefits), you are being social in the simple sense. If, instead, you arrange for a policy of first-come-first-served on the grounds of their approval of that as *they* understand it, your sociality is compound.[15]

A choice you make can be social simply and also social compoundly. Sometimes you can even arrange to get a choice to be social both ways, this by getting the others to see the options as you see them. Again, you are the President and are proposing a general health-care program. This promises to be fair and effective, but it will have to be centrally managed, and many people are uneasy with that. They know that the program is fair and would work, and they want such a program (one that is fair and would work), but they see it as socialized medicine, and as such they resist it. Here you must try to persuade them. Say that you get them to come around to seeing the project as you do. Since that way seen, they approve of it, your pursuing it would then be social simply and also compoundly.

All I have been saying has been just about *option* sociality, the agent wanting to take an option that ranks highest in the social valuation of his options. Sometimes we want to take an option whose *outcomes* stand highest in the social valuation of the *outcomes*. There we might speak of *outcome* sociality. Again, our concept of sociality is of the option sort only, and our examples (the proxy, the painter, the dialysis planner) all exemplify that.[16] But the reader may prefer to let "sociality" refer to both kinds.

The analogy of sociality and rationality suggests still further distinctions. We have assumed the agent to be fully certain of the others' values – this makes for sociality *under certainty.* We might speak of the same under *risk* where he assigns only some (non-1) probabilities to their having these or those values. We might speak too of sociality under *vagueness,* and perhaps even of sociality under *ambiguity.* I will keep just to certainty cases, but it may be that the others are more common.

4 FELLOWSHIP

Let us get back to people's reasons, to the *becauses* of what people do. The painter fixed on a style of painting because his wife wanted him to. He did that to spare her the pain of thinking her husband a man unsure of himself. He did it because he cared for her, because in fact he loved her.

The story might have been different. He wanted to give his wife what she wanted and knew that his settling down would do it, but suppose that this didn't move him. Say that what moved him to settle down was wanting to be rich – this and his thinking it would make him rich *plus* his seeing his change in those terms, in terms of the money (*not* in terms of his wife). What he did would still have been social, but we would not call it *loving.*

"Love" is a word that figures little in philosophical writings. "Altruism" is more common. An altruist sees the possible outcomes in terms of the welfare of others, and he wants these others well, happy, contented, etc. So the painter was altruistic: he saw what he did as pleasing his wife and he wanted to please her. But calling him an altruist would miss the whole poignancy of his story. He would have done the same if he thought his wife would not be pleased by it, if he thought that, after he did it, she would just be pained by something else. What was basic wasn't the thought of any good it would do her, but his thinking she *wanted* it done and his wanting to do what she wanted. That and his being moved by a reason taking in these grounds.

So the word "love" may be best. "Friendship" will serve in other cases like it, or we might use the word "fellowship." A person is moved by fellowship where what he does is socially grounded and he sees it in terms of the wantings, the values, of certain others. He not only wants to do what these others want him to do (or want *someone* to do) and thinks he is doing that, but he sees what he is doing as what these others want done.

Fellowship needs no illustration, but it may help to look at some cases. Something at least very like it appears in Richard M. Titmuss's study of the donation of blood.[17] Titmuss discusses the various methods of collecting blood in different countries, and he reports that blood donations in Britain are "the closest approximation in social reality to the abstract concept of a 'free human gift.' The primary characteristics of such donations are: the absence of tangible immediate rewards in monetary or non-monetary forms; the absence of penalties, financial or otherwise; and the knowledge among donors that the donations are for unnamed strangers."[18] Putting this more broadly, the donors (in Britain) gave blood because they wanted to help and knew that it would be helping and saw their action that way. Again, what led them to give? In their own words: "Knowing I mite be saving somebody life," "You cant get blood from supermarkets and chaine stores. People them selves must come forword," "A desire to help other people in need."[19]

This may seem an unclear case, for the donors (or those just quoted) were as much altruists as social agents. They were responding to what people needed as well as to what they wanted, most indeed thinking more about "helping" than about obliging the others. Still, this must count as love of one's neighbor if anything counts as that at all, and it suggests that the fellowship concept has to allow for some complex reasons. A person may see what he is doing in a certain conjoint way, as doing what others want to have done and also as giving them what they need. And he may now want to do both and think he is doing both. If without both these belief-desire-and-seeings, he would not be doing what he is, he has a double or complex reason to which his sociality is essential. We can let ourselves speak of fellowship in such cases too, and that marks the blood donors here (or many of them) as instances.

Another case of complex reasons, this one from Axelrod's book on cooperation. Axelrod describes the live-and-let-live system of trench warfare in World War I. The Western Front extended then for five hundred miles through France and Belgium and was the scene of much carnage. But on broad sectors and for long periods of time (until the British generals intervened), there was remarkable restraint on both sides. In certain sections, each side refrained from shelling the other during meal times. At one location, 8 to 9 A.M. was set aside for "private business": no shelling during that hour. Sometimes there was no shelling at all, aside from occasional volleys meant to make a racket without causing harm.

Axelrod reports the trench confrontation as a supergame of a Prisoners' Dilemma, and he discusses the live-and-let-live system as a rational tit-for-tat lock-in. But he mentions an "interesting development," the fact that the system eventually led to some "fellow feeling" between the two sides. He quotes a report of an incident in which

> . . . suddenly a salvo arrived but did no damage. Naturally both sides got down and our men started swearing at the Germans, when all at once a brave German got on his parapet and shouted out "We are very sorry about that; we hope no one was hurt. It is not our fault, it is that damned Prussian Artillery."[20]

Axelrod remarks that the German's apology goes beyond trying to prevent retaliation, that it reveals a concern for the others. A part at least of that concern looked to what the others wanted. The German had wanted his side of the trenches to hold its fire, as the English side wanted. And that (if only in part) is how he saw what his side had been doing: he saw it as what the English (all but their generals) wanted his side to do. The live-and-let-live system was no longer a rational policy only. It was altruistic (the German hoped that no one was "hurt"), and it was also (in our sense) social. It expressed the fellow feeling that then held between the two sides.

The system having developed among strangers and opponents, Axelrod takes it to be showing that "friendship is hardly necessary for cooperation . . . to get started."[21] He reports the incident of the salvo to show that fellowship "reinforces" cooperation. Still, he might have gone further. Friendship isn't necessary for cooperation to get started, but it is sometimes sufficient – more broadly, *sociality* is sufficient. Axelrod holds that, in some situations, rationality calls for cooperation, and often, in those cases, sociality does too. And sometimes sociality calls for it though rationality argues against it.

For instance, consider a Prisoners' Dilemma (as in Figure 1). Adam knows that Eve prefers his taking S to his taking T, that she *wants* him to take his S, for he knows that, whatever she does, she will be better off if he took S. (We might say that Adam knows that his S is *Eve*-dominant in this game.) Likewise, Eve knows that Adam wants her to take her S, this because, whatever he does, he will be better off if she took S. (She knows that her S is *Adam*-dominant.) Suppose that Adam and Eve are social vis-à-vis each other. Each then wants to do what the other wants him or her to do. Each knowing what the other wants, each will here take S, and that will yield $\langle S,S \rangle$, which is the cooperative outcome. That is, if Adam and Eve are social, they will both cooperate, and this though rationality directs them both to T.

Likewise in a supergame of the Prisoners' Dilemma (though rationality sometimes allows for cooperation in such games). Each of the parties knows that the other wants him or her to take S all the way (Taylor's option C^{∞}). If each is socially focused on the other, each will choose that option. That will yield $\langle S,S \rangle$ in every round, and so here too, if both agents are social, both of them will cooperate. Likewise also in Chicken, in the one-round game of that (Figure 2) and also in its supergame.

This doesn't say that social people cooperate here *because* they are social. Rational people don't do what they do because they are rational either. Being rational and being social are defined by the grounds people have, not by the reasons that move them, and so "becauses" don't enter: the grounds people have don't explain what they do. Still, there often is a connection, for the social grounds people have plus certain understandings provide them with reasons. Where social people see their options in terms of what others want them to do, they cooperate because of the special (social) reasons that they then have.

Social people don't always cooperate. Sometimes they can't tell what, if anything, the others want them to do (as in the turmoil of *Romeo and Juliet* and in Figures 3, 4, and 5). Sometimes people's being social points them *away* from cooperation (as in Figure 6). I have been speaking of Prisoners' Dilemma and of Chicken games only. In these, sociality implies cooperation. And in a one-round Prisoners' Dilemma, social people cooperate and rational people don't.

5 LOOKING AHEAD

We spoke in Chapter 4 of looking to our future selves' values. That too is a sort of sociality, our future selves standing as others to us. Likewise where the future selves won't be our own selves. But how can the future of other people figure in our thinking about what to do?

In theory at least, this isn't a problem, or at least not a new one. The future selves of other people are just more others for us, and we can attend to these others' futures as we do to our own. Some discounting may be called for on a probabilistic basis, taking account of the likelihood of someone today still living then, or on some different basis. (We might say, "That would no longer be Eve" or "Better a benefit sooner than later.") These "different bases" can be troubling, but we have spoken of that before.[22]

Should we look only to how these others will value the situations they will be in or also to how they will value our doing what led to their then being where they are? Should we attend to the regrets they will have, if regrets are what we foresee, and to their gladness in hindsight, if we anticipate that? We raised some questions like this before, in the one-person case, and we found no general answers.[23] There are no general answers here either. All depends on our present values, on how much the backward reactions of the others matter to us now.

We may encounter some boot-strapping here. The others may later endorse what we did because of values we induced in them by what they will be endorsing. Students obliged to learn a foreign language may develop a taste for it; they may then be glad of the policy that obliged them to learn it. A liberal (or a conservative) education often instills the sort of values that make the people it shaped be glad of their liberal (or conservative) schooling. It can happen the other way too, regret being boot-strapped instead of gladness. "Educations that encourage introspection and self-criticism may produce preferences that partially or wholly condemn the institutions that created such preferences."[24] Should we take such hindsight judgments into account in planning ahead? We asked the same question in the one-person case, and our "Why not?" carries over.

Still, there are complexities here. Think of cases of long-range planning, of institutional or ecological or population-growth planning. In these, the future others aren't later selves of people now alive: they won't be *born* until later. Here discounting is more of a problem.[25] We can't discount the future by the improbability of its being reached. We are thinking of times far ahead, but of people who, by assumption, will then be alive. Nor can we justify how we discount on the basis of our disavowals. "That person won't be *me*" is true of every one of these people. But that is a part of what makes for the problem, so it can't help to say it.

Boot-strapping too raises special problems. The values these people will have in their time may be contingent on what we do now – we have gone over this ground before. But there is a new twist here, for these later, yet-to-come people may themselves be contingent. Who will and who won't be alive in the future may depend on what we now do.

Say that we are debating some large-scale birth-control policy. If the policy is adopted, fewer people will be born. And since births will be differently spaced, many of those who will be born will be different from the people who would have been if we had followed no policy. (They will have different genes.) Looking ahead to some future day, could we ask whether our adopting the policy would be good for the people then alive – good in their own estimation – whether it would be better for them than our not adopting it? No, for who will then be alive will depend on what we do now, and so there is no fixed *they* or *them* whom we could either help or harm. Some authors conclude that this discredits all population-growth policies, and indeed all future-directed welfare programs of any sort.[26]

No need to draw that conclusion. There are two possible futures here: a crowded world and a sparser one. The people in the sparser world (possible people in a possible world) are happier than those in the crowded world, but it may be that those in each world prefer their own to the other, if only because they believe they wouldn't exist at all in the other. This recalls the Black Hills case (the job offer from Wyoming),[27] though that was a one-person story, the same person, same *us*, in both futures. We found two ways of looking at that, two questions to ask about it. So also here, where what is contingent is not our own future but future others – future people or whole populations.

Here too there are two questions. Which of our options has a prospect (outcome) that the people who would live in that prospect would rank no lower than the prospect of the other? This gives us a *no-grousing* analysis. Which of our options has a prospect that the people who would live in that prospect would rank no lower that the people alive in the other would rank that other prospect? This gives us a contentment or *happiness* analysis. (The rankings here are *collective* rankings, the rankings these people would have as groups.)

It isn't always obvious how we should answer these questions. Still, in the population-growth problem, a no-grousing analysis lets us take either of our options and a happiness analysis points us toward population control (if we think of a collective ranking as some sort of an average). As above, in the one-person case, I incline to the latter approach: Why not do what would yield the most happiness for the people who would be alive?

Here is a darker, less tractable problem. A woman is facing the issue of whether to have an abortion. If she does, the future others, or those she considers, will be those now alive; if she doesn't, there will be one more. Say that she knows that the child she would have would be a burden to her, that her self in the world without it would have been much happier. This may incline her to have the abortion. But she may also feel a commitment to the contingent infant. She knows that the child would want to live, and that may leave her troubled. In which of the possible futures before her would those involved, all in all, be the happier? (In which of these futures would the collective valuation of the then-world be the higher?) Or putting the question more narrowly, how should her burdened future self's misery weigh against her then-child's interests, against the value it would set on its being alive?

Things could be messier still. Change the woman's story a bit. Suppose that she doesn't want the child but that she knows that, if she had it, she would get to be happy with it, that she would be happier with it than she would have been without it. Here not only her child and its values but her own future values are contingent. Should she attend to her present self only or to others too, including that child who would exist if . . . *and* those later selves of her own who would be glad that they had that child? Or better, how ought she to weigh her interests, those she now has, against these others' – including the interests of her own later selves, including their *contingent* interests? To some, this question is easy: her interests trump all other people's and those she now has trump all. She herself may not be so sure. What are the rights and wrongs of this? The next chapter takes up some issues of rightness, but this is one question it won't try to answer.

7

CHOOSING RIGHT

THE knottiest problems remain. Should we always be rational? Why should we *ever* be rational? When should our choices be socially grounded? Also, what are good grounds to have? And what is a good *reason*? I have no answers to some of these questions, and to the rest only sketchy ones, but the questions can't be ignored.

1 WHY BE RATIONAL?

Our parents said, "Be rational!" Our friends say, "Don't be a fool!" But is there really an issue for us? Some people think that there isn't, that it isn't up to us. They say we all are bound to be rational, whether we like it or not. This must be looked into right at the start, for no need to try to be rational if we can't be otherwise. And no need to ask *whether* we should be or *why* we ought to be rational.

There are two approaches to the no-other-possibility thesis. The first is an *a priorist* approach. This begins with something like my concept of reasons above. I have held that a reason is a belief-plus-desire-plus-understanding. Where we are choosing x for a reason, we think that x is of sort y, we want to choose something of sort y, and we understand what we are choosing in the terms of y. We are reaching for something or other we think is of a sort that we want. In that sense, we are reaching for something that (we think) serves our interests. So too in cases of action: where we act on some reason we have, we are pursuing our interests.

The *a priorist* line now offers this way of thinking about being rational, that we are rational where we pursue our interests. And it asks us to accept this idea, that nothing counts as something we *do* unless we are moved to it by some reason. Where we aren't moved by a reason, we are being passive. We aren't agents of change in those contexts but only subjects (or loci) of it; what occurs there isn't our doing. Our choices and actions *are* our own doing. They don't just happen to us. So there are always reasons behind them. In them all, we pursue our interests, and so, in them all, we are rational. Whether our choices and actions are rational – whether we are rational in what we are *doing* – is therefore not up to us. It doesn't depend on *what* we are doing. It is implicit in the concepts of doings and reasons and rationality.

It is implicit in some concepts of them, but it isn't in mine. My concept of *doings* doesn't imply that the doer is moved by some reason. A choice is always our own doing, but it may be unreflective. It may have no reason behind it. Likewise for our actions: my concepts allow for thoughtless action, for acting on an impulse. What we are doing need have no reason, so the argument breaks down right there.

As for being rational – yes, a person being rational is pursuing his interests, if this means only that he is reaching for something that he wants. But the same holds for any person who has grounds for his choices and actions, whatever those grounds are. A rational person's grounds are distinctive; *what* he wants is distinctive. He wants to do what would come out best or has the best all-in-all prospects.[1] For contrast, recall the proxy's going by what his constituents wanted. Or think of the painter's settling down because his wife wanted him to. The prospects didn't figure there, only the wishes of certain others. That made these people what we called *social.* They wanted to attend to certain others; they did that, and so they did what they wanted – and in that sense, they served their interests. But this doesn't mean that these people were then being rational.

Let me say too that, as I define it, a person's being rational doesn't depend on his reasons, on those reasons in their fullness. It depends just on his grounds, on what he wants and believes. A person is rational where what he is doing rests on grounds of the best-prospects sort. He may have such grounds and have others besides. And perhaps these others here move him, the ones wired up by his understandings – that is, he may be moved by reasons that expand on these other grounds. The painter was moved by his wanting to do what he thought his wife wanted him to, but he may have also thought he would in the end be the better off for it – perhaps he thought she would leave him if he didn't. The proxy went by the vote, though he may have thought that he would lose his job if he didn't. If their thinking was mixed in this manner, taking in the wishes of others and also their own assessments of the outcomes, these people were social but they also were rational. Our grounds-based theory of rationality is broad: what we do socially may be rational too. It is not so broad, however, as to make all we do rational.

The second approach is different. It argues that what we do must be rational because we evolved on that basis – call this the *evolvist* idea. Our species was favored by evolution for our rationality, that making up for our lack of strength and agility, etc. So we must be rational, typically at least, or very often, though the *must*ness is not *a priori*. We *must* in the sense in which we must be resistant to the most common bacteria, the sense in which we must be immune to normal solar radiation: if we weren't, we wouldn't be here.

This gives being rational too much credit. Where people are being rational, they do what they think will come out best for them. But being rational allows for being wrong and for doing very badly. A rational person may be wrong in what he thinks the outcomes would be, and the outcome he takes to be best needn't be adaptive for him. It needn't connect with his real-life problems, with his actual circumstances: it needn't help him to make his way in them or even to stay alive. The people who manage to stay alive longest don't always do it by being rational.

Besides, evolution doesn't favor those who live the longest. It favors just the survivors. And whole people never survive, only their genes do – those of some people. Evolution favors the genes of people who get their genes reproduced, and thus it calls for people doing what they needn't think best for themselves. It calls for their having children, or at least nephews and nieces or cousins, and for providing for them, sometimes for risking their own lives for them. Those who are rational needn't have kin (and help to sustain them and keep them from harm), and those who are not rational may. Evolution then smiles on the latter, not on the former.[2]

Neither the *a priori* nor the evolvist argument proves what it claims to prove. Neither proves that we *must* be rational, always or typically or ever. This opens the door to the question of why (or whether) we *should* be rational, and the usual answer is that a person who isn't will be sorry. There is seldom an argument here; mostly we get instances. Still, there is one argument. This speaks just of Bayesian rationality and holds that, in the long run, that pays. It says that we ought to be Bayesian-rational wherever the Bayesian logic applies because those who follow that logic wind up being the better off for it.

Here, in brief, is that argument.[3] Suppose that a person thinks he will face the same kind of issues many times over: the same kind of options, the same sort of outcomes, the same utilities and probabilities. The expected utility of an option equals the long-run average payoff of options of that sort.[4] By always taking the option that maximizes his expected utility, the agent thus assures himself of having, in the long run, the maximum average benefit. So a Bayesian-rational agent can count on doing as well as he could.

This assumes a long run of issues. What of those cases in which we think the issue we face is unique? Or what if a person is getting old and thinks he won't face many more issues? Why should he reason the way he might if he saw a long future ahead? We can put these questions aside, for the long-run argument fails even where long runs are foreseen.

Why be Bayesian rational? Why maximize expected utility? Again, because our keeping to Bayes would leave us as well off as possible, given our options in the case: it would yield us, in the long run, the maximum average payoff. This cuts a lot of corners. Putting the corners back, we can say that the probability would be high – and the longer the run, the higher – that the value of the average payoff would be close to the maximum we could get.[5] There would be a small probability – in the long run, vanishingly small – that the average payoff would be less. The different possible long-run average payoffs of following the policy have different probabilities, and so we can make only this claim for it, that the policy has, in the long run, the maximum *probability-weighted average* payoff-value. Since the individual payoff-values are the utilities we set on the payoffs, it comes to this, that following the policy has, in the long run, the maximum probability-weighted average *utility* – the maximum *expected* utility. But this just says that the Bayesian policy is the one a Bayesian endorses, the policy a Bayesian would advise us to follow.[6] The question remains, why follow it? Why accept the advice?

The long-run answer to "Why be rational?" preaches to the converted. And so too would any other it-would-be-best-for-us argument. Such an argument tries to establish that being rational has the best prospects. If it does establish that, it has taken us half of the way. The second half is the harder part; that must show us that we should follow the policy whose prospects we think are the best. A person promoting rationality does of course say that we should, but he can't count on agreement there, for this *should* is what is in question. Taking agreement for granted on that would beg the question asked.

2 MORE ABOUT *WHY*

There are people who want us to be rational. (Our friends who say, "Don't be a fool!") Ought we to be rational because these people want that of us? That would argue for rationality on the basis of its being social. It would offer us social grounds for our being rational. It would not be preaching to the converted, for an appeal to being social doesn't imply an endorsement of being rational. Still, would such an appeal carry weight? It would if we agreed that we ought to be social. But perhaps that too is in question.

So let us turn to that. Why should a person be social? Why sometimes – why indeed ever? Why care about what others want? One answer is that they *want* you to care and that you know this about them. This gets us nowhere at all: it says that being social would be social. A second answer is that sociality pays, both in the long run and in the short. Being attentive to other people often gets you friends, and friends can be good to have, for they attend to you. This is the idea of reciprocal sociality: I rub your back and you will rub mine.[7]

Your being social is here promoted on the basis of its being rational, on the basis of the benefit you foresee its yielding you. (Your foreseeing a benefit from it doesn't undo your being social, no more so than your expecting it to gratify your friends undoes your being rational.) We have here a conditional or would-if justification of sociality: sociality's being rational would justify our being social *if* we could show that we ought to be rational. But this last we don't know how to do. So yes, being social (often) is rational, but that alone doesn't justify being social. And besides, we are now in a circle, promoting rationality on the basis of its being social and sociality on the basis of its being rational.

We are getting nowhere, perhaps because we are asking too much. Where we ask about sociality and note that being social is rational, must we also argue somehow that we ought to be rational? Say that we *want* to be rational. Why not let that settle it for us? And if we want to be social too, why not stop right there: Why bother to argue for being social in terms of its being rational? Likewise where we ask about rationality and note that being rational is social, and we *want* to be social. Why doesn't wanting that settle it? And again, why ask at all – why doesn't our wanting to be rational suffice?

Indeed, "Why be rational?" may be misleading. It sounds as if we were facing some issue, as if we had to choose between our being rational and not. But all of us want to be rational – at least very often, in many situations. Our minds are made up on that from the start. And we also fully expect to be rational much of the time. So we have no choice to make. We face no issue in "Why be rational?" (or at least none in "Why be rational often?") not because we *must* be rational but because we have no open and live options on that matter.[8] The trouble with "Why be rational?" is that it looks like a serious question, one that calls for an answer, but isn't. (Perhaps the only proper answer to it is "Why not?")[9]

So too, for most people, with sociality. Most of us want to be social sometimes, we *want* to want to oblige certain others, which means that we find no issue in why (or whether to) be social. We have no choice to make there either. Most of us therefore need no answer to the question "Why be social?" (aside from the basic "Why not?"). For some, perhaps there is an issue; but since those people want to be rational – I am supposing we all want that – they can think about "Why sociality?" in the back-rubbing way. They can note that the favors they do often get some return, that being social often pays, that it often is rational.

Still, if all of us want to be rational, why must we sometimes be *urged* to be rational? (Our friends again, with their "Don't be a fool!") And why are we sometimes applauded for it? Being rational is simple enough. We need only want to do what would have the best prospects for us and do what we think of that sort.

Why then should we be commended for choosing or acting rationally? So too about being social. Why do we often think well of a person for his social attending to others? And why do we sometimes fault him for this?

Take that painter again. What he did was decent and fine, but not just because it was social. We reflect on the whole situation: we are touched because he attended to that woman in that way. The woman, his wife, was not complaining. He sensed her distress and what would relieve it, and that got him to change. We might take a different view if she had badgered and bullied him. Or if the woman wasn't his wife, but was instead his *ex*-wife, living next door with his ex-best-friend. We might then call him a sap. We might say that he should have been firm, that he shouldn't have yielded on this, certainly not to her.

Or take some person debating what to do with a large sum of money. He looks into various investment opportunities and chooses the one he thinks offers him most. Or perhaps he is altruistic and thinks in terms of helping others and then goes for that. Either way, his choice is rational, and we would often say he did right. Still, in some cases we wouldn't. Suppose that the money wasn't his own. Suppose it had been given to him to distribute in certain ways and that he had promised to do this. He shouldn't then have thought of investing or of how he might do the most good, whether to himself or to others. He should have kept his mind on doing what he had promised to do.

Sometimes we should be rational. At other times, we shouldn't, or it isn't clear that we *should.* Sometimes a person ought to be social; sometimes he would be a sap. So the questions about being rational and being social remain, but their adverb has changed. They are no longer asking *why.* They are asking *when:* When should we be one and when the other, in which sorts of situations rational and in which sorts social? Our friends who urge us to be this way or that aren't giving us general guidance. They are addressing particular cases, the issues before us here and now. Still, some general rules are sometimes pressed on us too.

The rules are those of moral theory – of different, competing moral theories. When should we attend to others, and to which others should we attend? When should we go by what others want of us and when should what others want be ignored? Different theories offer different answers, some leaning more toward other-attending, some more toward autonomy.[10] Certain versions of Christianity are at the far extreme of attendance ("Not as I will, Lord, but as Thou wilt"). Some romantic self-proclaimings (Nietzsche's perhaps) are at the other extreme. Most moral theories are in-between somewhere, allowing both for being rational and for being social ("Attend to your friends and your family; aside from that, look out for yourself"). So there are many general rules, though there is little consensus.[11]

3 GOOD GROUNDS

Say that you ought to choose rationally in some situation, to choose on some rational grounds. You ought there to want what has the best prospects and to choose what you think of that sort. That tells you what you ought to want: you ought to want what has the best prospects. It doesn't tell you what you should think, that this or that option fills the bill. So it doesn't specify the grounds that you ought there to have.

Likewise, to say that you ought to choose socially isn't to point you to these or those grounds but only to grounds of a certain sort, to grounds that include your wanting to do what ranks the highest in your social valuation. Where you are choosing socially and we agree that you *should*, we are making a partial endorsement of certain grounds that you have; we are endorsing their desire component. To endorse those grounds *in toto* – to say they are *good* grounds for you – we would also have to endorse their component belief.

When is a choice well grounded? What counts as having good grounds? The general answer is obvious. It is that a belief-and-desire counts as good grounds for a person if he ought to have both that belief and that desire, or at least properly *might* have both. As this stands, no problem with it; everyone will agree. But what are the *oughtness* and *mightness* involved?

Do they refer to consistency only, on some large view of that? Or are they established by the real world, whatever we think it is like? Ought (or might) our beliefs be governed by the demands of inner coherence – by the demands of coherence alone, or ought we just to believe what is true? And regarding what we want: Ought we to want what our other desires (perhaps *inter alia*) commit us to wanting or ought we only to want what the real world somehow shows us is wantable?

We have here two different answers to our question about good grounds. One answer is *internalist*, the other answer *externalist.* Say that the belief and desire components of your grounds for this or that choice follow from other beliefs and desires. (Better, that what you believe and want follows from what else you believe and/or want.) The internalist says these are good grounds to have, that they are good grounds *for you* – even if, in his opinion, these beliefs and desires are wrong (if they clash with *his*). The externalist takes such thinking to be promoting mere self-delusion. (He sees it to be like trying to shore up your finances by lending yourself some money.) He holds that what makes our good grounds *good* is that their components reflect the real world.

I will be very brief on this matter. First, about internalism. Can that be the whole story? Perhaps it seems that we have to say *yes,* that we moved toward that from the start. Our theory of rationality is a subjectivist theory, and so is our theory of sociality. On the theories we have presented, nothing external to you (the agent) bears on what is rational and what social. What is one or the other for you depends on your beliefs and desires. But this says nothing about the question of what you *ought to* or *might* believe and want, of what defines *oughtness* and *mightness* here, and that is the question the internalist speaks to. Yes, we all are subjectivists, those of us who accept the preceding (in Chapters 3 through 6). But we needn't be internalists too. On that topic, the door was left open.

A special internalist problem is this. If our thinking needs to meet only the demands of inner consistency, why ever bother to read, to learn? We tell ourselves sometimes to look around more, to put off our choice until more facts are in. An internalist has to dismiss that. On his view, it doesn't matter how narrowly based (how thin) our grounds are. What counts is only how they cohere with our other beliefs and desires. That makes confirming them easy: if they fit in, they pass. (Should I think that chicken soup will cure this cold I have? Yes, because I think it is the cure for every illness.) But what if a person doubted his grounds and their credentials too? An internalist has to say that such doubts make no sense. An externalist disagrees; he holds that such doubts are fully proper and that only self-enclosed people never have such doubts.

For the externalist, the basic problem is to explain "reflecting the world." He holds that we ought to believe and to want only what is true or correct. That itself is modest enough, and common sense will accept it. But press the idea, and common sense falters. For what is truth: What makes something *true*? (It can't just be a correspondence to the world, for that would take us full circle.) And what role do our information, our background beliefs, our *evidence* play: Should we be held to believing the truth even if our evidence points us against it?

Also, what about what we want? When is what we are wanting right or proper or the like? Is it when what we want would be *good*? Good for just us, or good all around? And is that goodness, whatever it is, determined by "outside," external factors? Does nature ("the world") reveal what is good? The claim that it does goes back a long way, all the way back to the ancient Greeks, but so does the conviction that it doesn't.

We can pass these questions by. There is no lack of discussion of them, no shortage of studies of the goodness of grounds, of when beliefs and desires are right, of which we *might* have and which we *should*.[12] There remains an issue of rightness (of *oughtness*) that is seldom raised, and that deserves some attention.

4 GOOD REASONS

Suppose that our grounds for what we are doing are indeed good grounds. It doesn't follow that what we are doing is the right thing to do, nor that we will later be able to justify it or will have an excuse. The grounds that we had won't justify us or give us any excuses unless those grounds were a part of our reason, a part of what then moved us. And it also has to be that that reason was a good one to have – that we had a *good* reason.

If in fact we had good grounds and they were a part of our reason, how can the reason not have been good? Consider Macbeth again, after his wife got to him. He wanted to be bold (courageous, "manly") and he believed that the act would be bold. This belief-and-desire of his were his grounds for killing the king, and suppose these were good grounds for him, that he was right to have that belief and right too to want to be bold. (A Scottish chief had to be bold!) Still, his reason for doing it was this belief-and-desire he had *plus* his post-persuasion seeing of the action in terms of its boldness, and we may say that he shouldn't have seen it in that detached, impersonal way. We may say that he should have seen it as he saw it the day before, as a betrayal of trust – as the murder of his kinsman and guest. How he understood what he did (when he did it) was a part of his reason, and if that understanding was wrong, the reason he had was a bad one. But was his understanding wrong?

Here is a case from closer to home. Robert McNamara was secretary of defense for presidents Kennedy and Johnson. In his memoirs, he concedes that the Vietnam War was a mistake.[13]

He insists that those on our side who ran the war had the best intentions, that they wanted to preserve democracy, to stop the spread of communism. But he says that all these people, himself included, deceived themselves, that they ignored the obstacles in the way and exaggerated what would happen if the United States lost. He concludes that the people in charge shouldn't have thought the war was serving its purpose, that they all (himself included) lacked good grounds for what they were doing.

McNamara lauds what they wanted but faults the beliefs that they had. He says nothing about how these people understood the war. They understood it in political terms, in terms of treaties, of foreign policy. Those who protested saw it instead as a slaughter of innocents. They held that McNamara was blind to the misery and horror of the war, that how he saw things was wrong – they considered it *monstrously* wrong – and that therefore all he did was without a good reason. The reason he had was a bad one, and it would have been just as bad if all his beliefs had been right (if he hadn't deceived himself), if the grounds built into that reason had been good grounds to have.

Was MacNamara's understanding right or were the protesters right? Putting the question more broadly: On what does the rightness of an understanding depend? This is like our questions about the rightness (the "oughtness") of beliefs and desires. But the question has seldom been raised about people's understandings.[14]

Is there an internalist answer to it? Here is one suggestion, that the rightness of an understanding depends just on what is believed, that we are seeing something rightly where we see it as the conjunction of all we believe about it. If you believe that *x* and *y* and *z* . . . all report the same fact, you must understand that fact as *x*-and-*y*-and-*z* . . . .[15] On this *total information* principle, whatever you believe about some item enters into how you should see it. On this idea, McNamara was wrong, but so were the protesters – and so were Macbeth and the others. The way that they saw things was wrong, for they all focused selectively, seeing things in terms of only a part of what they believed about them.

Still, people often insist on the rightness of selective seeings. Think of a judge who is offered a bribe. He says, "That's a bribe, and I don't take bribes." His friend says, "It is a lot of money; it would be a *benefaction*. It is also a rare opportunity! OK, yes, it is a bribe, but see it as a bribe-*and*-benefaction-*and*-opportunity. That will bring out the pros and cons for you." The judge may well dismiss this advice. He may say he is duty-bound to see a bribe as just a bribe.

It could be argued that the judge is mistaken, that his being a judge doesn't bind him to seeing things in any narrow way, that it only binds him not to accept any bribes. This would mean that his being a judge constrains only how he chooses and acts and that the rightness of how he sees things might be governed by the total-information principle. If it were so governed, the judge could see the bribe he is offered as his friend urges him to, as a this-and-that-and-that. He would then be facing a problem under ambiguity (qua bribe, this isn't acceptable; qua benefaction, it is very nice . . .). But he still couldn't weigh and balance. He would have to think lexically, to reflect on first things first, the avoidance of bribes getting top priority, and this would go against our logic for ambiguity problems. So the total-information principle would exact a price.

The price to be paid would be heavier yet where there is risk involved. Take Kahneman and Tversky's risk scenario (in Chapter 3). The total-information principle obliges us there to see the outcomes as winding-up-with-500-not-including-sunk-gains-*and*-with-1,500-*including*-them, winding-up-with-a-loss-of-500-not-including-sunk-gains-*and*-with-1,500-including-them, etc. If we did see them so, and if we held, as economists do, that sunk gains don't count, we couldn't choose here in the light of the utilities we set on the outcomes as we would see them (in terms of sunk gains *inter alia*). We couldn't maximize the expected utilities wired up by our understandings but would have to think in some way that let us ignore the sunk gains we were seeing. This would go against our logic for choice problems under risk. Better to keep to that logic and thus to reject the total-information principle.

Back to the question of when things are seen rightly. Is there an externalist answer? We might be offered this total-*truth* principle, that a person is seeing things rightly where he sees them as the conjunction of all that is *true* about them, that if *x* and *y* and *z* . . . are all true of the same fact, we must understand that fact as *x*-and-*y*-and-*z* . . . . The problem with this is exactly the same as with the total-information idea. We can't adhere to the total-truth principle and also to some policy of selective attending – a policy like that of ignoring sunk gains. Or rather, we can't without rejecting our logic. Better to keep the logic and to reject the total-truth idea too.

Here is a possible third approach, a kind of passing the buck. This refers just to the understanding of *actions*; it says that an understanding of an action is right if the action, so understood, would be right. We can't accept this either, for it would mean that there never could be a right understanding of a wrong action – of an action that is wrong under a proper understanding of it. Think of Macbeth's initial understanding of the killing as a betrayal. That understanding wouldn't be right because the killing, so seen, wasn't right.

Could we say that a right understanding focuses on what is *salient*? We could, but that would just beg the question. We are asking what *makes* something salient, what leads us to say that this or that is, what warrants our seeing things as we do. Still, it may be worth attending to actual judgments of salience. We often know where people stand on specific cases, what they think of certain understandings – that they are right or proper or crazy. And we know also what people think about how certain *sorts* of facts should be seen. These latter, more general judgments they make express their *ideologies*.

Let us pause over this concept. An ideology is typically shared by the people in some group. It is a commitment to shape understandings, to discipline them, to bring them in line – these people's own and sometimes others' too. It imposes a uniform slant on how things are seen or not seen, or how they are seen in this or that context. Different ideologies prescribe different seeings, different selective understandings.

We spoke of the judge rejecting a bribe, refusing to think of the money. He also, we hope, put out of mind the effect of his rulings on the advancement of his career. The ideology of the law appears in the image of blindfolded Justice holding the scales. The blindfold says that judges and juries ignore what others are likely to see – the difference in wealth or power or status of the plaintiff and the accused, and also whatever personal interest they (the judges and juries) might have. It says that such matters never are noted, that they *may* not be noted. It says they don't count, don't weigh in the scales.

Or think of sunk costs and gains. A part of the ideology of economics is that sunk costs and gains don't count. (This is proposed by economists, but not for economists only.) A typical statement is that a sunk cost or gain "should play no role . . . in any subsequent decision, for regardless of what we do, that historical cost [or gain] has been incurred, and is inescapable and unaffected."[16] The same idea, more tersely put: "Sunk costs [and gains] are irrelevant to current decisions."[17] This ideology, like that of the law, calls for certain ignorings or *not*-attendings. Other familiar ideologies direct us to certain *always*-seeings – for instance, that of always seeing every person as a fellow human being.

Why this or that ideology? Why *should* a defendant's social status have no bearing on how he is treated? In the past, until modern times, there was no *should* of that matter. Why should sunk costs or gains be irrelevant; why should they be ignored? Those who side with Kahneman and Tversky hold that sunk gains should *not* be ignored. And why should we always see other people as fellow human beings? Why not sometimes, in some situations, as strangers or as enemies? All these questions expand on this one: Why this or that understanding? They just put it more generally: Why *always* (or never) see *x*s as *y*s?

There are authors who reject the question. They deny all point to asking how an understanding might be supported. They ask only how it might be explained, how perhaps some understandings serve to advance certain purposes. Or they ask about these understandings how they accord with these or those others, whether they are widely shared or are the sort of understandings accepted in this or that group. History may enter here, but right and wrong do not apply, for as these authors think of it, the world (as understood) isn't found; it is *made*. People whose understandings differ have shaped and now live in different worlds, and no judgments can be made of one world by those who live in another.[18]

I resist this libertine view, though I have no good case against it. In the end, it may win by default, but in the meantime I put it off. I hold that some understandings are wrong, that Macbeth's was wrong when he did it and McNamara's was too, that they shouldn't have seen the killings they were involved in as they did. I hold that other understandings are right – Macbeth's before he let himself go, the judge's (when he rejected the bribe), the *A*-and-*D* choosers' (ignoring sunk gains). Still, no doubt I will be told that these judgments have no force. They reflect only my own perspective, my own "partisan, angled seeing,"[19] and a person who sees things differently will just shrug them off. The question remains: Is that where it ends? Can a judgment of right understandings never have any warrant? Or can it be backed up somehow?

5 SOFT-HEADEDNESS?

Our understandings are often decisive. They wire up certain values we have, values that, if they hadn't been wired, would have stayed dormant, inactive. And different values, thus activated, may point us in different directions. This speaks of what gets us to choose and to act. So it is only psychology, though it isn't the mainstream kind.

I have implied that it needn't to be faulted, that this role played by understandings isn't only common but proper. Here we move beyond psychology, and some people hold back. They think the move too indulgent; they mark it as being soft-headed. Yes, understandings play a role, but only as silent partners, at least in the mind of any sensible person. For such a person adheres to logic, to the rules of consistency, one of which states that, if you believe that *x* and *y* report the same fact, you must value *x* and *y* the same. You must value the fact qua *x* the same as you value that fact qua *y:* you must value the fact the same whether you describe it as *x* or as *y.* We met this rule in Chapter 3 and called it Principle *S.* We referred to the constraint it imposes as that of *extensionality.*

Much of what we have been saying rests on the rejection of *S.* Were we right to reject it? Can we let ourselves set different values on what we think is a single fact – on what we think is the selfsame fact, differently described? I have supposed that the answer is *yes.* But was that being soft-headed? This divides into two questions for us: *Can* we reject *S,* and *should* we reject it? The first of these questions is easy. We can always reject a principle if no good case has been made for it. And I know of no good argument in support of *S.*

What might a supporter of the principle say? For a start, an obvious point: he can't follow David Hume. Hume was concerned with the principle of induction. What might justify *that*? Hume found no answer that satisfied him, and, in the end, he dismissed the whole problem. He held that induction is not up to us, that we are stuck with it, like it or not. He held that we are the sort of creatures whose actions in fact always go by induction, and that we needn't be able to justify what we are bound to do anyway.[20]

Perhaps this line was correct for induction. Perhaps that follows from human nature and thus is a practice we can't reject.[21] Not so for extensionality; the stories above all bring that out. Macbeth and the others went flat against it, which shows that it can be rejected, and so the question of why to keep to it can't be said not to arise. Hume called his treatment of his doubts about induction a "skeptical solution" of those doubts. That kind of solution can't be offered to someone who doubts extensionality.

Less yet could one argue for Principle *S* along Donald Davidson's lines. In Davidson's view, the principles of belief and of value (those that are basic) are *a priori*. They are implicit in our concepts of belief and desire and the rest: we *have to* think the principles true of people who believe *this*, who want *that*, etc. If we think Adam believes *x*-and-*y*, we have to think he believes *y*, for believing the conjuncts is part of what it means to believe a conjunction. If we think Eve prefers *x* to *y* and also *y* to *z*, we have to think she prefers *x* to *z*, for its being transitive is part of our concept of preference.[22]

This may work for some principles. Perhaps it works for Principle *T* – that if *x* and *y* are the same *object of valuation*, they must be valued the same. That principle, I noted, is beyond dispute, which may be all that a principle's being *a priori* comes to.[23] We can't say it works for Principle *S*, for since we here are disputing *S*, we can't think it *a priori*. *S*-extensionality is not implicit in our concept of values, and that rules out this easy approach to the question of why to keep them extensional.

The answer may be that it pays to do that. Here we turn to pragmatics. Perhaps if we keep to extensionality we will do better in the long run than if we don't – better in our own estimation. We considered such an argument in support of the Bayesian logic, and we saw that it didn't work. There have been other such long-run arguments,[24] and none of these has worked either. More to our present purpose, however, none has ever been offered for *S*.

Most of the recent pragmatic arguments take a strictly local approach. The long run doesn't figure in them. Their claim is that, if we keep to certain principles, we can at least have security; and that if we don't, we can't. These are the so-called money-pump arguments. They claim to prove that only an adherence to certain principles secures us against being pumped for money. I think that these arguments all fail too.[25] But again, and more to the point, I know of none like it for *S*.

One might perhaps try this. You prefer one outcome qua *x* to a second qua *y* but prefer the second qua *v* to the first qua *w* (and you know that *x* and *w* report the same outcome, and also *y* and *v*). To fix our minds on the situation, suppose that *x* and *y* refer to how much money these outcomes would yield you and *v* and *w* to their fairness or unfairness. Say that the issue has to do with the distribution of a legacy; *x* reports that you get a lot of money and *y* that you get very little, *v* that the legacy is fairly distributed and *w* that you get more than your share. Speaking in terms of *x* and *y*, some person now offers to arrange outcome one (to bring it about), for which service he asks a dollar. He plans then to switch to the *v*-and-*w* terms and offer to make it the second instead, for which he will ask another dollar. That is, he is asking a dollar to get you the better-paying outcome and is preparing to ask you for more for getting you the one that is fairer – and then to start all over. Are you about to be pumped?

No, or not necessarily. If you think in the *x*-and-*y* terms – if *x* and *y* put how you see what might happen, you will give him a dollar the first time. You will reject the second offer, having dismissed ("seen through") its wording. If you think in the *v*-and-*w* terms, you will reject the first offer but will accept the second. Either way, you will spend just one dollar and think it money well spent. You will not be a money pump. Of course, if he gets you to change how you see things every time he talks to you, he will be able to pump you. But that will then be because you are pliable, not because of any nonextensionality – not because you here go against *S*.

Clearly, this isn't conclusive. Perhaps a sound pragmatic argument for extensionality will yet be found. Or a different sort of argument will some day be made for it. Pending such a development, however, a supporter of extensionality is left treading water. He is left without a basis for his endorsement of Principle *S*. And for the rest of us, this much is clear: there is, at present, no argument for it.[26] So we are free to reject it.

We *can* reject Principle *S*. I think we *ought* to reject it, though here I can only repeat the case I have been trying to make all along. Rejecting the principle lets us attend to certain basic everyday matters – to ambiguity, to inner conflicts, to value rewiring and reversals. It lets us focus on them, and it lets us speak about them in a nondismissive way. It lets us say they are not just a nuisance, that they don't reflect lapses in logic. It allows for our making sense of how much we are preoccupied by them.

But must we speak of these matters at all, of ambiguity and conflicts and the like? True, they are common and can't be avoided. And our attempts to deal with them somehow are an important part of our lives. But no theory can take in all that. No theory can cover all life.

Still, a theory can cover too little. It can be too meager. Our topic here was how people choose, and how they *might* choose, and why. A theory of choosing is bound to take notice of our often starting divided, often in a conflict. And it must acknowledge also that we often stay conflicted after we have chosen, that we then (in that silent conflict) want all we wanted before. Perhaps the reader still likes to think that "purity of heart is to will just one thing." He can in that case take me as saying that we do better without it. And also that we are well off too for knowing how far we are from it.

NOTES

CHAPTER ONE

1. Lillian Hellman, *Scoundrel Time,* Boston: Little, Brown, 1976, pp. 53–54.
2. Bruno Bettelheim, *Freud's Vienna and Other Essays,* New York: Alfred A. Knopf, 1990, p. 29.
3. William Styron, *Sophie's Choice,* New York: Random House, 1976, pp. 483–84.

CHAPTER TWO

1. Both these ideas will need some refinement. We will get to that shortly.
2. This too will need some refinement, but the basic idea will stand.
3. This theory first appears in Aristotle's *De Motu Animalium,* 701[a]. For a worked out, recent statement, see Donald Davidson, "Actions, Reasons, and Causes," in his *Essays on Actions and Events,* Oxford: Oxford University Press, 1980.
4. See, in particular, Robert Jay Lifton, *The Nazi Doctors,* New York: Basic Books, 1986.
5. Ibid., p. 196.
6. Ibid., p. 195.
7. This speaks of reasons for actions only; we will soon make it more general.
8. The three-factor theory has deep roots too. I discuss them in my *Understanding Action,* Cambridge: Cambridge University Press, 1991, pp. 55–71.
9. Thus an action neither *is* nor *reveals* a choice. There may have been no choice whatever (Sophie pushing her daughter forward). Or the choice may have been of some option under an understanding we can't infer from what followed (as in the button/bomb story).
10. Notice that even intense desires can turn out to be weak. Also that

weakness of will may be common and that it isn't a character flaw. For more on all this, see my *Understanding Action,* pp. 110–15.

11. If different understandings don't distinguish different facts, what does distinguish them? On that question, see Donald Davidson, "The Individuation of Events," in his *Essays on Actions and Events.* But see also Alvin I. Goldman, *A Theory of Human Action,* New York: Prentice-Hall, 1979, Chap. 1.
12. Or we could speak of some aural matters. You might hear a chord as a chord, or as a G-major chord, or as a rolled chord, or as a *wrong* chord. These are four distinct understandings (different *seeings*?) of what the pianist is doing.
13. Both quotes are from *Macbeth,* Act 1, Scene 7.
14. In all these cases of being persuaded, one person is persuading another. Often we try to persuade ourselves and we find that not easy.
15. The basic difference between beliefs and understandings may perhaps be this, that beliefs (as also desires) are propositional attitudes and understandings are not; see my *Understanding Action,* pp. 71–84.
16. I do that in my *Understanding Action,* pp. 42–45, where I remark on some critics.
17. It is like the refinement I offer at the end of Section 4.
18. For Hume's discussion, see his *An Inquiry Concerning Human Understanding,* Sects. 7 and 8.

CHAPTER THREE

1. The demands of objectivity are discussed in Chapter 7.
2. We must also assume that the number of outcomes is finite. Otherwise every outcome might be bested by some other, leaving no best outcome even in the absence of cycles.
3. For more about that donkey, see my "An Indifferent Ass," in Leigh S. Cauman, Isaac Levi, Charles D. Parsons, and Robert Schwartz (eds.), *How Many Questions? Essays in Honor of Sidney Morgenbesser,* Indianapolis: Hackett, 1983.
4. I present a capsule history in my *Understanding Action,* Chap. 2.
5. The probability of *not* getting a double six in one throw of two dice is 35/36. That of not getting a double six in 24 such throws is $(35/36)^{24}$. That of getting at least one is therefore $1 - (35/36)^{24}$, which equals .4914.
6. On a more detailed analysis, the weights are the different proba-

bilities *conditional on the option's being taken*. Also, the valuations are of the outcomes *as the agent understands them*.

7. Some authors hold that being rational calls only for satisficing expected *utility*. For instance, see Michael Slote, *Beyond Optimizing*, Cambridge, MA: Harvard University Press, 1989.
8. The concepts of security and hope limits are studied in Isaac Levi, *The Enterprise of Knowledge*, Cambridge, MA: MIT Press, 1980; see esp. Chap. 7.
9. This needn't be the utility of $29.48, the utility of the expected *benefit* of the gamble. Where a gamble's expected utility is the utility of its expected benefit, you are being *risk neutral*. Where it is less, you are risk *averse*; where it is more, you are risk *inclined*.
10. Ramsey's analysis appears in his "Truth and Probability," first published in 1931 and reprinted in his *Philosophical Papers*, edited by D. H. Mellor, Cambridge: Cambridge University Press, 1990. For a simple and clear presentation, see Richard C. Jeffrey, *The Logic of Decision*, 2nd ed., Chicago: Chicago University Press, 1983, pp. 46–51. See also Nils-Eric Sahlin, *The Philosophy of F. P. Ramsey*, Cambridge: Cambridge University Press, 1990, Chap. 1.
11. I revise it myself in my *Having Reasons*, Princeton: Princeton University Press, 1984, pp. 20–23.
12. They follow if we assume that the utility of every proposition is a probability-weighted average of the utilities of certain conjunctions in which that proposition figures; see my *Having Reasons*, pp. 22–23.
13. On the neglect of complexity (ambiguity), see Amartya Sen, "Rational Fools," *Philosophy and Public Affairs*, Vol. 6 (1977), reprinted in his *Choice, Welfare and Measurement*, Oxford: Blackwell, 1982.
14. Suppose that, for every dimension, the utility of each outcome is unambiguous both under that dimension and under its complement (the juncture of all the others). Then Ramsey's derivation of probabilities suggests a way of measuring importance; see Richard C. Jeffrey, *The Logic of Decision*, pp. 46–50, and let p and $1 - p$ be importance weights. But the essential supposition about unambiguity only rarely holds.
15. For a variety of approaches to it, see Ralph L. Keeney and Howard Raiffa, *Decisions with Multiple Objectives*, Cambridge: Cambridge University Press, 1993, esp. Chaps. 3 and 5.
16. See note 14.
17. For more on this, see my *Having Reasons*, pp. 23–28.
18. For instance, see John Rawls, *A Theory of Justice*, Cambridge, MA:

Harvard University Press, 1971, pp. 152–56, though Rawls is speaking only of cases of vagueness "marked by certain special features."

19. Better, not *every* constriction; only those that generate points meeting certain conditions – for instance, that the sum of the (point) probabilities of x and of not-x be 1.
20. I develop this idea in my *Having Reasons;* see esp. pp. 23–24 and 43–45. A closely related concept appears in Isaac Levi, "On Indeterminate Probabilities," *Journal of Philosophy,* Vol. 71 (1974), and in his *The Enterprise of Knowledge.*
21. Reported in Daniel Kahneman and Amos Tversky, "Prospect Theory: An Analysis of Decision Under Risk," *Econometrica,* Vol. 47 (1979).
22. Ibid., p. 273.
23. Kahneman and Tversky's analysis is put most clearly in their "The Framing of Decisions and the Psychology of Choice," *Science,* Vol. 211 (1981), and in their "Rational Choice and the Framing of Decisions," in David E. Bell, Howard Raiffa, and Amos Tversky (eds.), *Decision Making,* Cambridge: Cambridge University Press, 1988.
24. Again, I use the word "facts" as a catchall for actions and events and situations and the like.
25. For Kahneman and Tversky on this, see their "Rational Choice and the Framing of Decisions." (A different position appears in Tversky's "A Critique of Expected Utility Theory: Descriptive and Normative Considerations," *Erkenntnis,* Vol. 9 [1975].) "Extensionality" is used as above in Kenneth J. Arrow, "Risk Perception in Psychology and Economics," *Economic Inquiry,* Vol. 20 (1982).
26. These are the people who *would* have chosen both *A* and *D* if they had been both in I and in II.
27. For the concepts of risk aversion and risk inclination, see note 9.
28. For more on sunk costs and sunk gains and the like, see my "Allowing for Understandings," *Journal of Philosophy,* Vol. 89 (1992); also my *Understanding Action,* pp. 129–39.
29. Could we consider the options the same *in essential respects*? No, for that would be begging the question. The question of which respects are essential is what divides the *A*-and-*D* choosers from the others.
30. I discuss the likely arguments in support of *S* in Chapter 7.
31. We should, I think, also accept Principle *U,* that if x and y are *logically equivalent,* they must be valued the same. Whatever value

you set on having an 80% chance of getting over some illness you must set too on having a 20% chance of *not* getting over it.

32. We might also put it this way, that what we value are *propositions;* see Chapter 2, note 15.

CHAPTER FOUR

1. Søren Kierkegaard, *Purity of Heart Is to Will One Thing,* New York: Harper, 1938, p. 27; the reference is to James 4:8.
2. Their being options means that the agent doesn't want them *as he understands them;* see Chapter 2, Section 4.
3. This point is stressed in Isaac Levi, *Hard Choices,* Cambridge: Cambridge University Press, 1986, Chap. 2.
4. Bernard Williams calls such cases "tragic"; see his "Conflicts of Values," in his *Moral Luck,* Cambridge: Cambridge University Press, 1981.
5. Adam in Ivan Klíma's novel, *Judge on Trial,* New York: Alfred A. Knopf, 1993.
6. In Chapter 3, Section 4.
7. Easier said than done; see Chapter 3, Sections 4 and 5.
8. In Ernest Jones, *Hamlet and Oedipus,* Garden City: Doubleday, 1954.
9. For this idea of weakness of will and some comments on inner struggle, see Harry G. Frankfurt, "Freedom of the Will and the Concept of a Person," in his *The Importance of What We Care About,* Cambridge: Cambridge University Press, 1988.
10. The open courses in such a conflict aren't options on our definition (the agent here wanting to take each course *as he understands it*), so these conflicts take us beyond what I announced as our topic.
11. Strictly, the values you had in the past also might enter, but let that go here.
12. One who did was Henry Sidgwick; see his *Methods of Ethics,* 7th ed., London: Macmillan, 1962, pp. 124n and 381.
13. This isn't in the story, but never mind.
14. For the concepts of avowal and disavowal, see Herbert Fingarette, *Self-Deception,* London: Routledge and Kegan Paul, 1969, esp. pp. 66–72. See also Harry G. Frankfurt, "Identification and Wholeheartedness," in his *The Importance of What We Care About.*
15. Derek Parfit, "Later Selves and Moral Principles," in Alan Montefiore (ed.), *Philosophy and Personal Relations,* London: Routledge and Kegan Paul, 1973, p. 145.

16. Robert Louis Stevenson, *The Strange Case of Dr. Jekyll and Mr. Hyde,* Harmondsworth: Penguin, 1979, p. 97.
17. Derek Parfit, "Personal Identity," *Philosophical Review,* Vol. 80 (1971), p. 25. Parfit expands on this idea in his *Reasons and Persons,* Oxford: Oxford University Press, 1984.
18. Jekyll would have agreed. He swung between the rejection of Hyde and the admission that "this too was myself" (Stevenson, *Dr. Jekyll and Mr. Hyde,* p. 84).
19. F. P. Ramsey, "A Mathematical Theory of Saving," first published in 1928 and reprinted in his *Foundations,* edited by D. H. Mellor, London: Routledge and Kegan Paul, 1978, p. 261.
20. The analogy of time preference and self-preference is made by Thomas Nagel, though for a different purpose; see his *The Possibility of Altruism,* Princeton: Princeton University Press, 1970.
21. For a discussion of pure time-preference (and conflict), see George Ainslie, *Picoeconomics,* Cambridge: Cambridge University Press, 1992.
22. That would then be a value "reversal," as in Chapter 3, Section 6.
23. On this, see Bengt Hansson, "The Appropriateness of the Expected Utility Model," *Erkenntnis,* Vol. 9 (1975).
24. That we get ourselves into circles is argued in Anna Kusser and Wolfgang Spohn, "The Utility of Pleasure Is a Pain for Decision Theory," *Journal of Philosophy,* Vol. 89 (1992).
25. I take the idea of ratification from Richard Jeffrey, though he applies it more narrowly; he lets it take note of our next selves' probabilities but not of their utilities or desires. See his *The Logic of Decision,* pp. 15–20.
26. My use here of "choosing *for s*" is not like that above (and in Chapter 6). There I speak of our choices being grounded in the values of the *s* we choose for (e.g., our cross-time self); here *s* just has a veto.
27. For how this bears on some recent conundrums, see my *Understanding Action,* pp. 121–29.
28. Gladness here is not the same as what we described as "being gratified." You are gratified (or disappointed) with what happens; you are glad of (or you regret) what you did to bring that about.
29. This deals with cases of certainty only. Also, both ideas ignore the possibility of later choices shaping still-later values; so some refinements are needed, perhaps refinements like those in Philip Bricker, "Prudence," *Journal of Philosophy,* Vol. 77 (1980), p. 397.

30. The Black Hills story is taken from Bricker, *op. cit.* I am here drawing heavily on that paper.
31. The gravestone of W. C. Fields announces, "Here lies W. C. Fields. He would rather be living in Philadelphia." Fields was unhappy in Philadelphia. Perhaps he is happier now, but he still is grousing.
32. Jekyll and Hyde weren't usual. Some other unusual (though real-life) cases appear in Kathleen V. Wilkes, *Real People,* Oxford: Oxford University Press, 1988, Chap. 4.
33. This question goes back a long way. See John Locke, *An Essay Concerning Human Understanding,* Bk. 2, Chap. 27, Pars. 9 and 10 (1690). See also David Hume, *A Treatise of Human Nature,* Bk. 1, Pt. 4, Sect. 6 (1739).
34. For the freedom and liveness conditions, see Chapter 2, Sections 1 and 4; for the dependence of choosing on options, see Chapter 2, Section 2.
35. For a more detailed argument, see my "Self-knowledge, Uncertainty, and Choice," *British Journal for the Philosophy of Science,* Vol. 30 (1979). This is reprinted (with some corrections) in Peter Gärdenfors and Nils-Eric Sahlin (eds.), *Decision, Probability, and Utility,* Cambridge: Cambridge University Press, 1988.
36. I mean here by our knowing our reasons our knowing *that they are* our reasons.

CHAPTER FIVE

1. Jean-Paul Sartre, *No Exit and Three Other Plays,* New York: Vintage, 1989.
2. That is, there is a joint scaling of the benefits that makes the sum come to zero.
3. Over the outcomes *as they see them.*
4. For some political applications, see Lester C. Thurow, *The Zero-Sum Society,* New York: Basic Books, 1980.
5. As they each see these two outcomes.
6. Given that the options of the others aren't probabilistically keyed to his, which we are assuming they aren't.
7. The commons story was first presented in Garrett Hardin, "The Tragedy of the Commons," *Science,* Vol. 162 (1968). For other such cases, let the commons be the forests, or the oceans, or the air we breathe.

8. The Cuban missile crisis was a real-life Chicken game, with $\langle T,T \rangle$ as mutual Soviet-American annihilation.
9. This is their ranking of the outcomes *as I have described them;* I am supposing that these people see the outcomes that way.
10. Each knows the others' rankings of the outcomes *as these others see them.*
11. This can't require Adam to know all that Eve knows about *him.* For then he would know that about himself, and this could run afoul of what we said in Chapter 4 about the bounds of self-knowledge.
12. A vast amount has been written on this. Useful surveys appear in R. Duncan Luce and Howard Raiffa, *Games and Decisions,* New York: Wiley, 1957, and in Ken Binmore, *Essays in the Foundations of Game Theory,* Oxford: Blackwell, 1990.
13. It is called a *Nash* equilibrium, after John Nash's analysis in his "Non-cooperative Games," *Annals of Mathematics,* Vol. 54 (1951).
14. In many theories, the blankness condition figures as part of the definition of games.
15. Suppose that both T,S and S,T are equilibria in some two-person game, Adam preferring $\langle T,S \rangle$ to $\langle S,S \rangle$ and being indifferent between $\langle T,T \rangle$ and $\langle S,T \rangle$. Here T is dominant for Adam, so the S,T-equilibrium is excluded.
16. More generally, where there are more than two options, a person may have dominated options without having any that is dominant, and the others, knowing this and deleting those options, may find that they have dominated options of their own in the truncated game.
17. For a very different analysis of the several-equilibria problem, see John C. Harsanyi and Reinhard Selten, *A General Theory of Equilibrium Selection in Games,* Cambridge, MA: MIT Press, 1988.
18. Every two-person game can be expanded into one that has an equilibrium pair by giving each agent a set of options containing every probability mixture of his initial options. But this then is not the initial game, which needn't have had equilibria.
19. The last clause goes beyond what is usual. Even joint actions that benefit all are here *not* cooperative if everyone might have done still better, or if someone might have done better without any person doing worse.
20. A Prisoners' Dilemma this way arrived at has sometimes been called an *Altruists'* Dilemma.

21. Figures 8 and 9 don't reflect the costs of enforcement, so these may be wrong from the start.
22. For Taylor's analysis, see his *The Possibility of Cooperation*, Cambridge: Cambridge University Press, 1987, an extensive revision of his *Anarchy and Cooperation*, London: John Wiley and Sons, 1976.
23. See Chapter 4, Section 4, the cases of Hellman and Hamlet. (Hellman was resolute and Hamlet was not.)
24. There can also be superchoices that are not choices of supergame options: there can be superchoices in one-agent situations. For a theory of one-agent superchoices, see Edward F. McClennen, *Rationality and Dynamic Choice*, Cambridge: Cambridge University Press, 1990.
25. Paul Samuelson calls it "An eye for an eye and a kiss for a kiss, but start with a kiss."
26. I here follow Taylor in focusing on the discount *factor*, not the discount *rate;* the discount *rate* is 1 minus the discount *factor*. In other contexts (in Chapter 4), I follow the usual line of thinking of discounts in terms of *rates*.
27. The full analysis calls for assigning utilities to $\langle S,S\rangle$, $\langle T,T\rangle$, $\langle S,T\rangle$, and $\langle T,S\rangle$. It assumes that the utility of $\langle S,S\rangle$ exceeds half the sum of the utilities of $\langle S,T\rangle$ and $\langle T,S\rangle$; this provides for ranking the outcome of B,B above that of B,B'.
28. On Taylor's analysis, J,J would lead to B,B, the outcome of which would be $\langle S,S\rangle$, $\langle S,S\rangle$, $\langle S,S\rangle$, ... And we know that I,I would yield $\langle T,T\rangle$, $\langle T,T\rangle$, $\langle T,T\rangle$, ...
29. *Anarchy and Cooperation*, pp. 32–33; see also Taylor, *The Possibility of Cooperation*, p. 78.
30. B,B is the W-V pair in which $m = 0$.
31. There are other option pairs like W^m,V^m. In G^m, Adam tit-for-tats until there have been m successive S,S's; after which he takes T and then tit-for-tats again until there has been another row of m S,S's, etc. In H^m, Eve forgives a T by Adam provided it comes after m successive S,S's; apart from that, she tit-for-tats. G^m,H^m too may be an admissible equilibrium.
32. I expand on the discussion in this section in my "Cooperation and Contracts," *Economics and Philosophy*, Vol. 8 (1992).
33. This isn't the whole of the blankness concept; see Section 3 of this chapter.
34. This is reported in his *The Evolution of Cooperation*, New York: Basic Books, 1984.

35. Ibid., p. 41.
36. Ibid., p. 44.

CHAPTER SIX

1. Their knowing that their agreements are binding means that their games (and those below) aren't like our games in Chapter 5.
2. The usual definition of a *core* applies only where the outcomes yield some tranferable benefit (like money) to the agents. See Luce and Raiffa, *Games and Decisions,* pp. 192–95.
3. Think of Chicken, in which all three cooperative outcomes are in the core.
4. Kenneth J. Arrow, *Social Choice and Individual Values,* 2nd ed., New York: John Wiley and Sons, 1963, p. 17.
5. The main approaches and their basic results derive from Arrow, *op. cit.* (1st ed., 1951). A comprehensive survey appears in Amartya Sen, *Collective Choice and Social Welfare,* San Francisco: Holden-Day, 1970 (reprinted, Amsterdam: North-Holland, 1979).
6. Again, see Arrow, *Social Choice and Individual Values,* and Sen, *Collective Choice and Social Welfare.*
7. See, for instance, Robert Sugden, "Maximizing Social Welfare: Is It the Government's Business?" in Alan Hamlin and Philip Pettit (eds.), *The Good Polity,* Oxford: Blackwell, 1989. See also David Gauthier, *Morals by Agreement,* Oxford: Oxford University Press, 1986.
8. For the philosophical rationale, see Gauthier, *Morals by Agreement.* This line of thinking goes back to the second of John Locke's *Two Treatises of Civil Government.*
9. Rousseau's basic discussion appears in his *Social Contract,* esp. Bk. 1, Chaps. 6–7, and Bk. 2, Chaps. 1–3. For Devlin's position, see the essays in his *The Enforcement of Morals,* Oxford: Oxford University Press, 1965, esp. "Morals and the Criminal Law."
10. I am supposing that the others all are inner-integrated. Where they are inner-divided, there can still be some *micro*sociality, a responding to others' part-selves.
11. This will be conceded by all – call it the principle of *nonmalice,* that "if one [option] rises or remains still in the [valuation] of every individual without any other change in those [valuations], . . . it rises, or at least does not fall, in the social [valuation]" (Arrow, *Social Choice and Individual Values,* p. 25).
12. A number of writers have noted the analogy of social and inner-self integration; for instance, see Ian Steedman and Ulrich Krause,

"Goethe's *Faust*, Arrow's Impossibility Theorem and the Individual Decision Taker," in Jon Elster (ed.), *The Multiple Self*, Cambridge: Cambridge University Press, 1986.

13. The problem of finding a choice rule here gives way to that of establishing social valuations.
14. Sociality and rationality also can conflict, the agent there wanting to be social and also rational and thinking he can't be both. So he may sometimes have to choose – to choose which way he will be.
15. The dialysis problem is based on an actual controversy when dialysis was first introduced; see Guido Calabresi and Philip Bobbitt, *Tragic Choices*, New York: Norton, 1978, pp. 181–89.
16. Strictly, in proxy's case, the option/outcome distinction fails, this because the proxy's options are themselves outcomes (of junctures of actions).
17. *The Gift Relationship*, London: George Allen and Unwin, 1971.
18. Ibid., pp. 88–89.
19. All these are in Titmuss, *op. cit.*, p. 227.
20. Owen Rutter (ed.), *History of the Seventh (Services) Batallion, The Royal Sussex Regiment, 1914–1919*, London: Times Publishing Co., 1934; quoted in Axelrod, *The Evolution of Cooperation*, p. 85.
21. Axelrod, *The Evolution of Cooperation*, p. 87.
22. See Chapter 4, Section 3.
23. See Chapter 4, Section 4.
24. Tyler Cowan, "The Scope and Limits of Preference Sovereignty," *Economics and Philosophy*, Vol. 9 (1993), p. 257. Cowan's paper raises issues closely related to those here.
25. On this topic, see Tyler Cowan and Derek Parfit, "Against the Social Discount Rate," in Peter Laslett and James S. Fishkin (eds.), *Justice Between Age Groups and Generations*, New Haven: Yale University Press, 1992.
26. For instance, see Thomas Schwartz, "Welfare Judgments and Future Generations," *Theory and Decision*, Vol. 11 (1979).
27. See Chapter 4, Section 5.

CHAPTER SEVEN

1. I will be speaking in this chapter of one-agent rationality only.
2. This assumes the modern theory of evolution as the selection of genes. A useful, popular exposition appears in Richard Dawkins, *The Selfish Gene*, Oxford: Oxford University Press, 1976.
3. It can be traced to Condorcet; see Isaac Todhunter, *A History of the*

Mathematical Theory of Probability, New York: Chelsea, 1965, pp. 392–93.

4. This (roughly) by the Law of Large Numbers.
5. The Law of Large Numbers provides for no more.
6. Strictly, our Chapter 3 Bayesian policy isn't to maximize expected utility but to do what we *think* would maximize. Still, this can't help the argument.
7. It resembles the sociobiologists' concept of reciprocal *altruism,* though that is often reported as just a tit-for-tat rational strategy. The initial source is R. L. Trivers, "The Evolution of Reciprocal Altruism," *Quarterly Review of Biology,* Vol. 46 (1971).
8. For the openness and liveness conditions, see Chapter 2, Sections 1 and 4.
9. This has to do with best-prospects rationality. What about equilibrium-rationality? Most people are not preinclined to that, so whether, in games, to move for equilibria might be an issue for them. This means that the question "Why equilibria?" remains.
10. I develop this idea of moral theories in my *Having Reasons,* Chap. 6.
11. There remain some why-questions here: for instance, why should we accept theory *x* and not theory *y*? The theories themselves don't provide any answers.
12. What makes believing this or that right is the main topic of epistemology. What makes *wanting* something right is a large part of ethics.
13. Robert S. McNamara, *In Retrospect,* New York: Random House, 1995.
14. For a brief history of the question, see my *Understanding Action,* Chap. 5.
15. Again, I use the word "fact" very loosely, as a kind of catchall.
16. Armen A. Alchian, "Cost," in Harry Townsend (ed.), *Price Theory,* 2nd ed., Harmondsworth: Penguin, 1980, p. 232.
17. Hal R. Arkes and Catherine Blumer, "The Psychology of Sunk Costs," *Organizational Behavior and Human Decision Processes,* Vol. 35 (1985), p. 126.
18. For this idea, see Nelson Goodman, *Ways of Worldmaking,* Indianapolis: Hackett, 1978. See also Richard Rorty's writings, esp. his *Contingency, Irony, and Solidarity,* Cambridge: Cambridge University Press, 1989.
19. This nice phrase is Stanley Fish's, whose position this is too; see his

There's No Such Thing as Free Speech, New York: Oxford University Press, 1994.

20. For Hume's discussion, see his *An Inquiry Concerning Human Understanding,* Sects. 4 and 5.
21. Hume speaks of induction as "a species of natural instincts, which no reasoning . . . is able . . . to prevent." This ignores his own objections to finding *musts* and *can'ts* in nature; see Chapter 2, Section 6.
22. Davidson writes, "The satisfaction of [these principles] . . . may be viewed as constitutive of the range of applications of such concepts as those of belief [and] desire" – this in "Psychology as Philosophy" in his *Essays on Actions and Events,* p. 237.
23. It may work too for the stronger Principle *U,* which holds that, if they are *logically equivalent,* x and y must be valued the same; see Chapter 3, note 31.
24. For instance, Hans Reichenbach's argument for induction in his *Experience and Prediction,* Chicago: University of Chicago Press, 1961, pp. 348–57.
25. I show how they fail in my "Dutch Bookies and Money Pumps," *Journal of Philosophy,* Vol. 83 (1986).
26. It could be argued in support of *S* that we can show it to follow (for utilities) from the definition of expected utilities. But putting a modest proviso on the definition blocks the derivation of *S.* See my "Allowing for Understandings" and my *Understanding Action,* pp. 90–93.

INDEX